Jugoslavia
120 km / 75 miles
AUSTRIA
HUNGARY
ROMANIA
BULGARIA
JUGOSLAVIA
ALBANIA
GREECE
ITALY
Adriatic
Gr. Glockner 3798
Bad-Gastein
Tauern-tunnel
Mur
Graz
Fürstenfeld
Jennersdf.
Balaton
Balatonboglár
Solt
Szeged
Arad
Crisul Alb
Deva
Dobbiaco
DOLOMITES
Villach
Klagen-furt
Drava
Maribor
Nagykanizsa
Szekszárd
Mureşul
Tržič
Varaždin
Pécs
Subotica
Timisoara
Belluno
Udine
Sava
Ljubljana
Zagreb
Barcs
Virovitica
Sombor
Tisa
BANAT
Timişul
Petroseni
Piave
Treviso
Trieste
Karlovac
Sisak
Osijek
Zrenjanin
Vršac
Tîrgu Jiu
Venezia
Golfo di Venezia
Piran
Rijeka
Novska
Sl. Brod
Novi Sad
Biograde
Dunav
Drobeta-Turnu Severin
Craiova
Smederevo
Rovinj
KRK
Plitvicka jez.
Plitvice
Banja Luka
Tuzla
Lazarevac
Pula
CRES
Bos. Petrovac
Vrbas
Zvornik
Vidin
Pto-Garibaldi
Mali Lošinj
Gospič
D. Vakuf
Ravenna
Titovo Užice
Paračin
Zadar
Sarajevo
Zap. Morava
Rimini
DUGI OTOK
Šibenik
Uśce
Niš
Vraca
Petrohan 1438
KORNAT
ŽIRJE
Neretva
KOPAONIK
S. Marino
Split
Mostar
Ancona
Žabljak
Bijelo Polje
Sofija
Arezzo
BRAČ
Fabriano
Perugia
VIS
HVAR
PELJEŠAC
Metković
Priština
KORČULA
Nikšic
Juž. Morava
Kjustendil
S. Benedetto
APPENNINO
LASTOVO
MLJET
Dubrovnik
Titograd
Struma
Drini
Orvieto
Gran Sasso d'Italia 2914
Skadarsko jez.
Skopje
Terni
Pescara
Petrovac
Shkodër
Solunska Gl. 2540
Vardar
Viterbo
L'Aquila
Lezha
Termoli
Kulata
Civitavecchia
Avezzano
Debar
Roma
Vieste
Gevgelija
Durrës
Tirana
Lido di Ostia
Frosinone
Campo-basso
S. Severo
Golfo di Manfredonia
Bitola
Foggia
Ohridsko jez.
Prespansko jez.
Thessaloniki

Dobro nam došli!

Imagine having a good friend who—having visited Yugoslavia numerous times—now knows the country like the back of his hand. This expert companion is going to show you around the bustling Adriatic coast, filling you in on all the important details as you go. This friend is, naturally, familiar with all the major sights, but also knows some special places off the beaten path. He has carefully worked out for you a series of itineraries and tours, based on his own personal recommendations and experiences.

Your friend and companion, the author of this book, is Hartmut Topf, a journalist who has repeatedly reported on the culture and history of this multi-ethnic state. Visiting the country each year since 1974, he regularly attends festivals and conferences, and helped to find Yugoslavian artists to take part in Berlin's 750th anniversary celebration. Together with architecture students from Berlin, he visited Budva after its destruction by an earthquake. He even helped to open up Berlin's partner city of Split for tourism, along with its hinterland and the islands Hvar and Brač.

This book offers advice and a guiding hand for those wishing to explore the Adriatic coast, either with or without a car. This fascinating coastal region bears the impressive marks of geological events and of human endeavour. It is characterised by a dramatic array of folds, steep cliffs and karstic hollows. There are waterfalls and caves to be explored, along with humble chapels and majestic cathedrals. Fortress ruins stand sentinel over rivers and ravines. All of this linked by the 'Adriatic Magistral', the main coastal highway and one of the world's most beautiful panoramic roads.

Insight Pocket Guide: Yugoslavian Adriatic is meant to stimulate your curiosity and to offer practical advice. Travelling in Yugoslavia remains an adventure as the country undergoes transition from a one-party state to pluralistic democracy. Even so, you will find a warm welcome wherever you go from the people of Yugoslavia, who are renowned for their hospitality: welcome to Yugoslavia!

Dobro nam došli! Welcome!

Insight Pocket Guide

YUGOSLAVIA

First English Edition

Printed in Singapore by:
Höfer Press (Pte) Ltd, Singapore
Fax: 65-861 6438

INSIGHT POCKET GUIDES

Yugoslavia's Adriatic Coast

Author **Hartmut Topf**
Publisher **Hans Höfer**
Design Concept **V Barl**
Designer **Willi Friedrich**
Photography **Oliver Lentz**
Managing Editor **Christopher Catling**

INSIGHT POCKET GUIDES

Contents

What to Know

Maps

Dear Reader!

My first encounter with Yugoslavia was in the spring of 1974. My research as a journalist brought me to Tito's country. I encountered a socialist federated republic which had just passed a new constitution and was not a member of the Eastern bloc—rather it emphasised its independence and non-alignment. It had just begun its hopeful efforts to put workers' self-administration into effect. Back then, Yugoslavia, to me, was the most complicated country in Europe and it has never been boring since.

I was particularly fascinated by the marvellous landscape, rich in contrasts; by a wealth of cultural monuments going back millennia; by a history preserved in stone of numerous ethnic groups and powers—and, naturally, by the people. On my first trip I only managed with the help of an interpreter, a native writer who soon became my friend.

Equipped with a tent, a car and a bare minimum of travel advice, I soon set out to pay this country a second visit—of a private nature this time. It proved to be a tremendous adventure. After many a tortuous path through the mountains and deep ravines of the interior, I finally reached the culmination of my journey: the road along the Adriatic, from the very southern tip at Lake Skutari up to Istria. Coming to the end of my trip and taking stock of my experiences with the country and its people, I realised that I was only at the beginning of a long relationship—not always an easy one, but one which would eventually mature into loyal affection.

Back home in Berlin I went back to school, trying to learn Serbo-Croatian. This went quite well for a while—but soon my heartache was to begin. What linguists regard as a single language is no such thing to the Yugoslavians. I am not merely referring to the fact that Slovenian and Macedonian are both languages in their own right; for all the factors which Serbian and Croatian have in common, there are still plenty of significant differences of vocabulary, literary style and phonetics.

All the same, I have kept at my Serbo-Croatian . . . or Croato-Serbian, persevering in my efforts to respect the many differences—even in the pronunciation of the national language. And the people have rewarded my efforts a thousandfold with their friendliness—people like the mechanic who mended a small defect in my car and—as a contribution to the friendship between two nations—refused to accept payment. Chance meetings by the roadside have resulted in a mutual trip to a museum or an invitation to enter a shady garden; an inquiry as to the content of a poster resulted in my attending a particular festival for many years to come.

The whole host of my Yugoslavian impressions is often overwhelming. What surprises me is how much people know about their ancestors, about their local history; all the anecdotes buzzing around involving robbers and rulers, romantic couples and rioting peasants—intertwining astonishing truth and well-spun yarn. Many of them combine dreams of present happiness with complaints about current problems: the economic crisis during the last few years, the plague of inflation which now seems, at last, to have been brought to a standstill, the transformation of the political system in Yugoslavia. These issues—and the football results—stir the hearts and emotions.

Then there is the tourist trade: a huge industry which often fails to exercise due prudence in its exploitation of the country's culture and natural resources. But those are not the only resources which seem inexhaustible; there is also the native population's talent for improvisation, its cordial helpfulness and sense of hospitality—these are all invaluable assets to a tourist industry that dominates the entire coastal region.

The curious guest who spends even a few days on the coast will benefit from this friendliness. You might also fall in love with the country, with a particular place. In which case you will gladly overlook the less pleasant aspects of the cities here: inadequate hygiene, noise, chaos, kitsch and mercenariness. Love has to be blind sometimes. And someone like myself is drawn to a great love time and time again.

HISTORY

The Struggle for Power

The eastern coast of the Adriatic was inhabited as early as the New Stone Age. This is proved by archaeological finds near Pula and Biograde, on Hvar Island and in Ston at the base of the Pelješac Peninsula. The names of earliest recorded settlers go back to 11th century BC sources: the Illyrians, Liburnians, Dalmatians, Japods, Vardaians and Pirustians. The entire Balkan Peninsula is an ancient cultural region. The Greeks began establishing colonies on the islands of Vis, Hvar and Korčula in 389BC; Togir was also founded then. Around a hundred years later the area was the scene of the first power struggle between the Greeks and the Romans. The evidence of this is found in Risan on Kotor Bay. By the first

Culture

century before Christ the Romans had subjugated the ruling tribes of the coastland and penetrated far into the Greek-dominated hinterland. In the year 6BC they founded the colony of Dalmatia with Salona—later Solin, north of Split—as the capital of their new province.

The spreading of Christianity was accompanied by the establishment of new provinces of the Imperium Romanum. During the years between AD295 and 305 the Emperor Diocletian erected his splendid palace by the sea in Spalato, the present-day Split. Following the formal recognition of Christianity by Constantine the Great in the year 313, numerous churches and monasteries were founded in the province. With the division of the Greater Roman Empire into a western and an eastern domain, the region along the eastern Adriatic coast went to Byzantium. In AD425, Christianity was declared the state religion; a few years later the Western Roman Empire collapsed.

Ostrogoths migrated into the region and conquered the coastal cities, waging war with Byzantium for 19 years. Even the Lombards had an interlude as conquerers, but with little lasting success. The first Slavs began settling the Balkans in 599. By this time the tribes had already begun to evolve into the ethnic groups which still exist today: the Bulgarians in the southeast and in the area of present-day Yugoslavia, the Serbians, Macedonians, Slovenes, and Croatians. In 788 Istria became part of the Frankish Empire.

The struggles for power between Rome and Byzantium, and the schism of the Church into an Eastern Orthodox church and a Western church of Roman Catholic observance, gave rise to countless armed conflicts, uprisings and permanent feuds over regional church sovereignty and the payment of tribute. Under Charlemagne a process of feudalisation began in the North, during the course of which the subjugated Slavic tribes in Pannonia and Dalmatia were Christianised. A Croatian diocese was established in

The city wall at Kašteca

Nin, also the seat of the Croatian duke. Having begun to gain ascendancy during the early 10th century, the Croatian state was now able to exact tribute not only from the Byzantine Adriatic cities, but also from Venice. In 925 Prince Tomislav was crowned the first Croatian king, his empire included Dalmatia and Pannonia.

During the following centuries, the Venetians repeatedly waged campaigns against the thriving cities along the Adriatic. The designs of arriving Normans and crusaders were anything but peaceful. The Serbian Nemanjid dynasty conquered the Zetan empire around Kotor and Budva along the southern part of the coast. Even rapacious Tartars got as far as Klis and Trogir. Countless were the feuds between the cities of the old state, between the aristocracy and the middle class, between feudal lords and peasants. The Croatian dynasty founded by Prince Trpimir during the 9th century did not survive for very long. After King Tomislav's victory over the other newcomers on the scene, the Hungarians, his empire extended from the Adriatic to the Drava (Drau) and had become an important military and political factor in Europe at the time. Nevertheless, in 1090, for lack of an heir to the throne, the Croatian dynasty became extinct.

The twelve Croatian tribes then gathered in the *pacta conventa* and decreed the fusion of Croatia with the Hungarian state. One result of King Koloman's combined rule over Hungary and Croatia was that it gave the Magyars free access to the sea. In the end, this part of what is now Yugoslavia would remain part of the Austro-Hungarian Empire for a long period. German-speaking scoffers called this great empire 'Kakanien', a word similar to that for 'cacophony' and to the German word for excrement. Be that as it may, the Empire had considerable impact in the Adriatic coastal region. The sweeping military success of the Turks in the Balkans left the Croatian feudal lords hardly any other choice but to replace the Hungarian regency with the patronage of the Habsburgs.

Having already received its own statute in 1272, Dubrovnik then became totally independent as the Republic of Ragus in 1358. This was the year of the signing of the Peace of Zadar, in which Venice relinquished all claims to the eastern coast of the Adriatic. But the Turkish Wars, the rivalry for succession between the the Houses of Luxembourg and Anjou, the disastrous crusade against the Bogumiles Bosnian sect, forced Vladislav of Naples, of the House of Anjou, to sell all of Dalmatia to Venice for 100,000 ducats, causing the Luxembourger Sigismund to abdicate to the feudal lords.

After partial successes against the Turks, the major powers continued their rivalry until Napoleon overthrew the mighty Republic of Venice in 1797 and founded the Kingdom of Italy, adding Istria, Dalmatia and Dubrovnik to the new state in the Peace of Pressburg in 1805. Upon Napoleon's defeat, his Illyric provinces (the region occupied by his troops eventually included the entire eastern coast of the Adriatic) fell back to the Austrians, who then in turn proceeded to support Italian hegemony over the Slavic population along the coast.

The Vienna Convention of 1815 and the Berlin Convention of 1878—banning the Turks from Bar and Ulcinj and recognising the new state of Montenegro—provoked the development of a Slavic liberation movement, which, despite numerous detours, eventually led to the founding of a state for all Southern Slavs. At the end of the First World War, the collapse of Austro-Hungary, along with its rule throughout most of the Balkans, made it possible for the Serbians, Croatians and Slovenes to amalgamate into one kingdom—which in 1929 was given the name Yugoslavia. Invaded by the Germans in 1941, it waged its 'war of people's liberation' until 1945 when the new state was founded.

The Communist Party of Yugoslavia, with Marshall Josip Broz Tito at the helm, had led the partisan war against the German and Italian occupation. The Communists combined the military war effort with a programme of Socialist revolution, triggering off radical social change whose repercussions are still felt today.

Roman temple site

The Current Situation

The current political changes in Eastern Europe are having their effect on Yugoslavia. The events of 1990 demand an assessment of the political status quo in Yugoslavia. The origins of the state as it was created right after the First World War—the Kingdom of Serbians, Slovenes and Croatians, cemented together, as it were, out of pieces of the Habsburg and Ottoman Empires and named Yugoslavia a few years later—put the country on shaky ground historically from the very start. Politically, the Republic—born out of the Occupation, the partisan underground and civil war—has also had to withstand many an earthquake. Tito's 'War of Liberation' united rival ethnic groups and minorities for the time being. Under this surface of 'brotherhood and unity', however, there was a society charged with explosive conflict. The system of socialist workers' control evolved into a form of institutionalised self-deception. Living on borrowed money, the country invested in ambitious but often absurd industrial projects, while supporting a huge throng of official loafers and minimally competent 'self' administrators at all levels of the economy and public life. Being a source of much-needed foreign currency, tourism underwent rapid development—unfortunately not always maintaining the right sense of ecological balance or respect for the traditional ways of life which are an integral part of the native culture.

Tito was not just a leader with a glorious past and a penchant for uniforms. The legendary Comrade's international reputation as a statesman, his leading role in the movement of non-aligned nations, secured him the the peoples' admiration long after his death. But criticism is growing among the country's political and cultural intelligentsia. The Yugoslavian League of Communists, the leading force for decades, is undergoing change—and breaking apart in the process.

Particularism and political pluralism are gaining ground—with Slovenia and Croatia paving the way in the spring of 1990. These regional republics—and their new, democratically elected governments—have taken on the task of transforming the Yugoslavian federation into a confederation of autonomous states. At this point, whether they will succeed or not is anybody's guess. However, the traditional, intensely national-oriented forces within the political spectrum are on an upward trend—there has been an increase in ethnic confrontations, both in number and intensity. The political turbulence has also reached the coastal regions of Slovenia and Croatia where tourism is most highly developed: Istria, Quarnero/Kvarner Bay and Dalmatia. In the hinterland of Central Dalmatia, not far from the coast, there is a Serbian minority of 600,000 people living on Croatian territory. As an expression of their desire for autonomy, they have also resorted to means which are anything but peaceful—whereupon the state government intervened with special police. Unnerved tourists fled from the holiday region in droves.

Even the less violent events involved in this process of transformation can have an effect on subjects covered in this book: street signs, for example. Many of the political names of streets and squares will disappear. So will the large, complex, cartel-like commercial organizations: quasi state-run or nationally-owned businesses, hotel and restaurant combines; they will become independent entities, selling off yacht harbours and athletic centres to new investors. Perestroika, Yugoslavian-style.

Private competition is a challenge to Socialist inefficiency; people are willing to pay for quality. The names of certain agencies, tour operators, restaurants and hotels will change; so will faces: there will be new owners and new personnel. State-sponsored, prestigious festivals are in financial jeopardy. The adjective 'socialist' is being removed from constitutions and from the names of government, starting with the regional republics. In Croatia, the Red Star once adorning the tricolour flag and policemen's hats has already given way to the white-and-red chequered pattern of the traditional coat of arms. You used to see the official portrait of Tito hanging in every ice-cream parlour and office throughout the country. Now, often you only see the tell-tale spot where the picture once hung . . . or else a new face in an old frame.

After years of disastrous inflation, the national cur-

rency has been made convertible. This means that Yugoslavia is no longer a cheap playground for guests from more affluent countries. At the moment, it is impossible to tell whether the central government's hard economic line will give the country the required stability, or whether Slovenia and Croatia will pursue their own concepts. There are bank notes currently in circulation which appear the same but have different face values. When dealing with the older bank notes you have to mentally 'cross off' the last four zeroes. The old 5,000 dinar note bearing the portrait of Tito (reduced in real value to half a dinar) was withdrawn from circulation in the summer of 1990. State subsidies for public transport and cultural institutions have been reduced. In times such as these, we have decided against listing prices in our book. Yugoslavia is a country where people have learned to improvise, which also has its own particular charm.

Tour Sel

Each year, Yugoslavia's Adriatic coast attracts large numbers of holiday-makers from all over the world. The scenic attractions, the traditional hospitality, its rich, highly varied cultural heritage, unspoiled nature, a wide range of tourist services, cultural and sporting events as well as good travel connections have favoured the development of the tourist trade during the last few decades.

Insight Pocket Guide: Yugoslavian Adriatic focuses your attention on four towns of major interest along the coast. These cultural centres serve both as orientation and as starting points for a series of suggested itineraries: excursions into the hinterland, as well as tours of the offshore islands.

Pula is the most interesting base for the northern section of the coast. Legend has it that it was founded by Jason and Medea. As a haven for refugees, it used to bear the name Polai. The Romans transformed it into their *Republica Polensium*, leaving behind splendid buildings. Many famous people have stayed here: James

ections

Joyce, Robert Koch, Franz Léhar and Thomas Mann, to name but a few. The huge amphitheatre, the Arena of Pula, is also the symbol of the annual film festival.

You have a choice of several excursions to places near Pula—for example to **Lipica**. This is the world-famous stud farm where the Royal Spanish Riding School used to obtain its noble animals. Look for **Postojna** (the Adelsburg Grotto) on the way. If you prefer a drive along the coast, try **Rovinj** and the **Limfjord. Motovun, Vodnjan, Piran** and **Poreč** are also worth a visit. And while you are in Pula, you should not miss the group of islands called **Brioni**—Tito's long-time residence. Via Labin there are various routes to new impressions: by ferry to the islands of **Cres** and **Lošinj**, to the music evenings of Osor, for example; by way of Opatija or through the hinterland to Rijeka for a visit to the opera and then on across the Tito Bridge onto the island of **Krk**.

From **Senj** with its old walls you can follow the main coastal road, the Adriatic Magistral, on along the foot of the mighty Velebit mountain range into the heart of Dalmatia. You can reach the island of **Rab** by ferry. This also applies to Pag Island, but the

city of **Zadar**, our next base, offers a more comfortable and interesting way of reaching this island.

Zadar, the breeziest of the larger cities along the coast offers a wealth of art treasures and impressive buildings. As a centre of heavy shipping activity the town provides ready access to a widely-scattered selection of islands. The neighbouring region around **Biograde** offers resorts, campsites and holiday villages, including a tourist village of exemplary quality to the north of town. Here you will also find the largest discotheque on the coast. From Zadar the most enticing excursion takes you to the islands of the **Cornati** archipelago, and this itinerary should also include the **Plitvice** lakes. Cornati and Plitvice are national parks. The island of **Pag** is worth visiting for its barren beauty and famous cheese.

The next centre is **Split**, a major city, harbour, industrial location and athletic centre of international importance. At the heart of the town is the Diocletian Palace with its temples and churches, vaults and narrow streets. Inviting destinations in the hinterland are historic **Salona**, the fortress of **Klis** and the city of **Sinj** with its medieval pageant. Along the bay, a string of towns called **Kaštela** mark the way to **Trogir** with its art collections and architectural gems.

Continuing our drive, we arrive in **Šibenik** with its traffic-free old town, the host of the annual international Children's Festival. Those interested will find additional tours from here: to the **Krka** waterfalls and to the **Visovac** monastery on a riverine island, and via **Murter** to the Cornati—if you have not already visited this archipelago from Zadar. From Split **Omiš** is easy to reach—a former pirates' roost where the best Dalmatian singing groups gather for a contest each summer and where the Cetina, rich in fish, flows through the tall mountains into the sea. If you would like to skip the drive into the hinterland, into the area around Sinj, you can cross over by ship from Split to **Hvar** or **Brač** or to one of the more distant islands, such **Vis** or **Lastovo**.

Although there are dozens of holiday resorts all down the coast to the Albanian border, the ideal base for the southern area of the Yugoslavian Adriatic coast is **Dubrovnik**. This is a very old city—much older than was assumed until a couple of years ago. The 'Pearl of the Adriatic' and Venice's perpetual rival, this republic maintained a clever balancing act between the major powers. Within its impressive fortress walls you will find a 'living museum', a rich cultural life and countless restaurants. From here you can pick excursions to the botanical garden, the arboretum of **Trsteno**, through the rich agricultural area of **Konavlje**, to **Ston** and across the isthmus to the **Mljet** Peninsula.

If **Lokrum**, the offshore bathing island (with, among other amenities, a nudist beach and a botanical garden), does not fit the bill, you could take one of the tour boats to **Cavtat**. Other jaunts out of Dubrovnik do not have to take you as far as **Mostar,** for there are any number of inviting places for a stop along the way, such as **Metković**, **Čaplina**, **Počitelj** and the Neretva Delta with its fruit vendors. Tempting destinations to the south are Montenegro, particularly **Kotor Bay**, the cities of **Kotor** and **Budva**, the hotel city of **Sveti Stefan** and high up in the mountains the old capital, **Cetinje**, and the mausoleum on the peak of Lovćen Mountain.

Pula

Pula is the first stop on our itinerary and the starting point for our exploration of the northern section of the Adriatic coast, the Istrian peninsula and Quarnero (Kvarner) Bay. This will also be the starting point of additional excursions and explorations. This city is to be preferred over Koper, located right next to Trieste, or Rijeka, at the beginning of the Adriatic Magistral.

History

Pula is considered to be the oldest city on the eastern Adriatic coast. According to ancient Greek sources going back to the third century BC Jason and Medea are given credit for founding the city on their flight from Colchis with the stolen Golden Fleece. In the vicinity of Pula archaeologists have found traces of human civilization going back 40,000 years; on the Brionic Islands they found the remains of Stone Age settlements and the remains of Cyclopic walls. The name *Pola*, or *Polae*, probably meaning 'castle' or 'well', came into being sometime prior to Roman times. In the year 40BC the city became a Roman colony. It was a seafaring centre and the export of wine, olive oil, wood, grain and cattle allowed Pula to thrive. The monumental Arena was erected under Emperor Vespasian and remains the city's emblem through to this day.

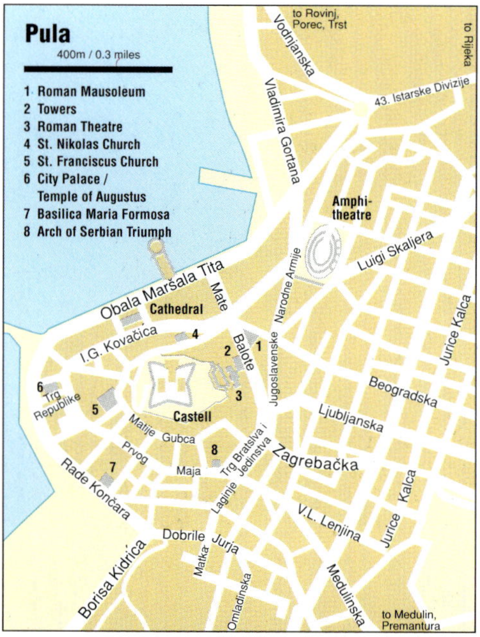

After the Christian victory in 425 Pula became a diocesan town. With the schism of the Roman Empire, it went to Byzantium and was conquered first by the Visigoths and then by the Ostrogoths. The Venetians sacked Pula, taking numerous art treasures. In 1797 Austria took power. German became the official and Italian the colloquial language. At the end of the World War I, Italy conquered Pula, staying until 1943. After a brief occupation by Germany the city was liberated by the Yugoslavian army in 1945.

The Roman amphitheatre

Tour 1

A Walk Through History

The oldest city on the eastern coast: Roman temples; Franciscan church and monastery; the impressive Roman amphitheatre; dinner at a fish restaurant. One day.

Why not spend your first day in Pula taking in the most interesting squares and buildings on a quiet stroll around town. Whether you are staying at the **Hotel Riviera**—rich in tradition and located near the train station, the bus station (*Kolodvor, Autobusni kolodvor*) and a stone's throw from the colossal Arena—or in one of the modern seaside bathing hotels or holiday centres in the area, you should be sure to get an early start to see the city at its quietest and to avoid the heat of the middle of the day—let's say, between 7 and 8am.

Coming from **Rudjer Boškovi'c** Park, south of Ulica Jurja, or via the main avenue (which is not packed with strollers until the sun goes down), the **Trg bratstva i jedinstva** (Square of Brotherhood and Unity), you will find yourself approaching the busiest place in town at this time of day. The 'piazza', the market on **Narodni trg** (People's Square)—with its booths, kiosks, open stands and an impressive, two-storied covered market—is just the place to feel the

pulse of Pula, to get a taste of the place. Speaking of 'taste': you might sample the cheese, buy some fresh fruit or try a portion of *burek*, a warm puff pastry filled with fresh cheese (*sir*) or apples (*jabuka*). The kiosks are stocked with foreign newspapers, bus tickets and various useful things. In the *bife*, or stand-up cafés, they will already have started serving schnapps, but an expresso may do you more good, or a *kapučino* (*sa šlagom*) with whipped cream, which is every bit as good as Italian cappuccino.

Now that you have got your circulation going, it's time for some stimulating history. **Ulica V I Ljenina** (Lenin Street—still!) will take you to the **Arch of Serbian Triumph** on the **Ulica Prvog Maja** (Street of the First of May). Salvia Postuma Sergi had this beautiful monument built in 31BC in honour of her three brothers. The inscriptions on the pedestals acclaim the commendable deeds of these three Roman administrators. This architectural gem, with its Corinthian semicolumns, appears as a favourite motif in the sketch books of Michelangelo, Palladio and other painters and architects. Its 'city' side is richly ornamented; its other side was the so-called *porta aurea*, the main city gate, until it was torn down in 1829.

If you take a few steps to the left to No 16 on the Street of the First of May, you can study the Roman mosaic which was discovered in 1959 during excavation work for a new building—on the former site of a luxurious city villa. Surrounded by ornamentation, the middle section of the mosaic portrays a scene from Greek epic. A woman named Dirka or Dirke is being punished for committing a heinous deed.

The area in front of the arch used to be a large Roman cemetery—which Dante refers to in the Ninth Canto of the *Divine Comedy* where he is describing hell. Now turn left onto **Ribarska Ulica** (Fisher Street). At the end (at the corner of Ulica Rade Končara) you will find the **burial chapel** belonging to the **Basilica Maria Formosa del Canetto** which once had three naves. Except for the chapel all that is left of the church is the north wall and part of the northern rotunda. Venetians presumably wreaked this destruction in 1243, scavenging columns and marble ornamentation to use in the building of San Marco.

Outside the city walls of the Roman Capitol some of the ancient buildings have remained standing. Today the Roman Forum is named **Trg republike** (Square of the Republic) and here you will find the **Temple of Augustus**—although built at the beginning of the first century AD, it is still in surprisingly good condition. Both the emperor and the goddess Roma were worshipped here—as you can read for yourself on the tympanum frieze.

A second temple, dedicated to the goddess Diana, has all but disappeared. All that remains, the rear wall of the inner room, was integrated into the mediaeval town hall, the City Palace. Originally dating back to the 13th century, this building—although considered to be Gothic—was continuously rebuilt well into the 17th century. The column-supported balcony completes the overall picture of the square in a dignified manner. No one knows how many buried treasures, what remains of the Roman era, may still lie hidden.

Crossing the square toward the south, you walk another few steps along the Street of the First of May before turning left into the ascending alleyway **Ulica** (or Uspon) **Balda Lupetine**. This will take you to the **Church of St Franciscus** and the associated 4th-century monastery. The tremendous Gothic basilican church was added in 1314.

You may want to take your time studying the elaborately ornamented church portal and the lovely rosette window above it before going inside to examine the extraordinary Gothic winged altar by the Pulan master Jakov and a carved and splendidly painted Madonna. You should have a look at the monastery courtyard—this atrium is an oasis of silence. In the monastery's St John Chapel you will find a Roman mosaic, and a 'lapidarium' in front of the Church of St Francis has several particularly pretty pieces of ancient masonry on display.

Here the **Ulica Matije Gupca** (Matije Gupca was the leader of a peasant uprising during the 16th century) circles the Castle Hill, so you have to decide, depending on the current temperature, whether you care to follow this street to the orthodox **Sveti Nikola** (St Nicholas) **Church**. The church houses an ikonostasis carved by Greek masters in 1705—however, it is often closed.

Aristocratic manot house in Pula

If you enjoy a bit of a hike and are not too tired, then you can head on up to the fortress: the little street is called **Uspon muzeju Narodne revolucije** and it actually does take you, via a series of stairs, to a museum dedicated to the Revolution and to the partisan struggle for people's liberation. You will need a half an hour to take a look around; the museum contains, among other things, documents and maps from World War II.

If the museum is closed, I suggest a walk around the outside of the walls. On the far side from the entrance there is a view inside a Roman summer theatre right behind the **Archaeological Museum**. The mountain itself was once the centre of the Illyric settlement, then of the walled Capitol of the Roman city. A fort dominated the peak in the 13th century, and what we see today are the remains of a Baroque fortress, a citadel with four bastions dating back to the 17th century.

Returning to the foot of the mountain, you can now head through the passage **Raspar organov uspon** to reach the **Cathedral** which is on **Ulica Ivana Gorana Kovačića**. The Cathedral of St Mary rests on the foundations of a temple to Jupiter—many elements going back to the 4th and 5th centuries have been preserved. The open roof construction is most impressive. The free-standing belfry was erected in the late 17th century; the Renaissance portal from 1457 belonged to the Church of St Michael which was part of a vanished Benedictine abbey.

The main altar of the cathedral is a sarcophagus carved with a praying figure. If you let your eyes wander across this church's outer walls you will discover many stone fragments going back to the early middle ages and several Latin inscriptions. There are Roman capitals serving as fonts, Roman mosaics set into the floor and the belfry is partially built out of stones from the amphitheatre.

You now have an opportunity to look out across the sea, down at the ships and the dockyards in the bay adjacent to the seaside promenade, the **Obala Maršala Tita** (Marshall Tito Embankment). This view may not strike you as especially romantic, although fishing boats sometimes take part in the scene.

Now walk on towards the arena, but do not hurry, for by now it really is time for a refreshing break. About this time of day a *gemišt* is just the thing—a mix of half white wine and half soda water—the Yugoslavian version of a spritzer.

It's up to you whether you let this be the aperitif before lunch or a light snack, or whether you walk the remaining few steps

Ruin of the Maria Basilica

down to the Arena. For there, you have the choice of resting either at a street side café or in the cool cellar under the mighty amphitheatre. Here you will find a permanent exhibition about wine-growing and olives and how they were processed in Roman times.

Speaking of wine and olives, if you have not yet stopped for a lunchtime snack, it is high time to treat yourself to some, or to one of the other specialities served in the neighbouring restaurants. Afterwards I advise you to head back to your hotel for a siesta. The natives always enjoy a rest after lunch—and not only on hot summer days—and the shops usually close around noon, the banks an hour later.

St Nicholas church

We then meet around 5pm back at the Arena—gorgeous in the afternoon and evening light—to continue our exploration of town. This first-century amphitheatre is the most impressive example of Roman architecture on Yugoslavian territory. The Emperor Vespasian built it to fulfill the wish of his girlfriend Cenida, a native of Pula. A smaller amphitheatre had existed at this site, going back to Emperor Augustus.

This mighty oval with an elliptical ground plan of 435 by 345ft (132 by 105m) rises to a height of three storeys. Due to the sloping terrain, the land side has two levels and is 78ft (24m) high. 23,000 spectators once gathered here to watch rapacious animals and gladiators fight for their lives. The Venetians made a quarry out of the theatre and even wanted to tear it down entirely to rebuild it on the other side of the Adriatic. Today, opera, concerts and the annual summer film festival draw an international audience. There are guided tours of the Arena in various languages. If you are in luck you may be able to take in an orchestra rehearsal or watch work in progress on a stage set.

Trg oslobodjenja (Liberation Square) between the Arena and the Harbour Captain's Building is where all tour group and agency coaches park; and from here the public service busses leave for neighbouring towns and holiday villages. The municipal buses stop on busy **Ulica Jugoslavenska narodne armije** (Street of the Yugoslavian People's Army) in front of the Arena. It is this one-way street which you now walk along, against the flow of traffic, until you can cross **Velikana Park** (*velikana* meaning 'giants' in the sense of 'the famous') on your right. On **Ulica Mate Balote** you will find the foundations of an octagonal mausoleum from the last century BC. On the opposite side of the street you can still see the remains of the old city wall. The double gate, the *porta gemina*, is

particularly beautiful. It leads to another more modest gate, beyond which you will find a flight of steps which lead upward to the **Archaeological Museum of Istria**.

The Augustus Temple, the church treasures and the Arena have already given you a strong, perhaps even overwhelming impression of this city's ancient cultural heritage. The Archaeological Museum will help you complete the picture. Plan to stay an hour, perhaps even longer— it is worth studying the many finds from earliest prehistoric times, and from antiquity through to the middle ages, to get a picture of the historic continuity of this part of Europe and of the city of Pula. In the summer the museum is open until 8pm.

Once you have had your fill of the treasures in the Archaeological Museum, I recommend following the city wall to the end, passing the **Hercules Arch** and then finally arriving in the **Korso**. In the twilight hour throngs of people pass by under the old trees lining the avenue. This is where youngsters meet and where families come to stroll; there are plenty of cafés, restaurants, news kiosks and taxi stands.

For dinner you can either drive or ride (bus No 2 or No 4, or by taxi) to the popular **Ribarska koliba fish restaurant** on Verudela Peninsula or spend a relaxing evening with good food and music in one of the cafés or hotels right here.

To see what is on the Cultural Summer programme for the evening, or to check upon the evening's offering of ethnic music and dance performances and concerts, discotheques and dances, you can refer to the leaflet in various languages put out by the Tourist Association each month and which is available free of charge at all hotels, tourist agencies and marinas.

Accommodation

Hotel Brioni
Pula
Seaside hotel
Tel: 34 888

Tourist Association
Pula, JNA 13
Tel: 052-24062

Top Portorož
Wide-spread organization,
Hotels and excursions
Tel: 066-73235

Arenatourist Pula
A Smareglia 5
Tel: 052-23811

Emona Globtour
Trg bratstva i jedinstva 10
Tel: 052-41255 or 23266

Kvarner Express
Obala Maršala Tita 14
Tel: 052-22519

Atlas
P. Drapšina 1
Tel: 052-33486

Tourist Association Umag
Tel: 51363

Hotel Piran
Piran, very pretty.
Tel: 066-73651

Tourist Association Rovinj
Tel: 052-811566 or 813469

Hotel Organisation Poreč
Plava Laguna
Tel: 053-31811

Tourist Association Mali Lošinj
Tel: 051-861547 or 861713

Tourist Association Cres
Djure Salaja 11
Tel: 051-820833

Hotel Kimen
Cres
Tel: 051-871161

Agencies

Kompas
Tel: 051-771484

Atlas
Tel: 051-771586

Restaurants

Amfora
A Rismondo 23, Rovinj
Tel: 052-815525

Kotlič
Pizzeria, Beogradska 10, Rovinj
Tel: 052-813106

Miscellaneous

Brioni National Park
(Administration), Fažana
Tel: 22455

Lipica
Stud farm and hotels
Tel: 067-73781, 73792 or 72617

Police/Emergency
Tel: 92

Ambulance Service
Tel: 94

Hospital
Zagrebačka 34
Tel: 33433

Tour 2

On Horseback and a Wondrous Cave

Horses and riding in Lipica (Lippiza); Postojna Cavern, an underground wonderworld with a subterranean concert hall; Piran, a charming resort. One day.

If you have just left Pula by car or are on your way to Istria from Ljubljana or Trieste and are looking for a bit of pleasant diversion, you do not have to be a serious speliologist or dressage rider to be fascinated by two special places: **Postojna** and **Lipica**.

You can reach Postojna directly via the motorway connecting Ljubljana with Istria; and Lipica is only a short distance from the Italian border. The nearest border town is Sežana, but you had best go by way of Lokev—there are better direction signs and the road is in better condition. Another bit of advice: when driving from Postojna to Lipica, I recommend you take the Lokev route: the signs are better, so you cannot possibly get lost.

Lipica is the original stud farm of the Lippizaners, the famous white exhibition horses associated with the Royal Spanish Riding School at the Burg Theatre in Vienna. Lipica has specialised in horse breeding and dressage since 1580. There are two good hotels with every amenity imaginable: tennis courts, an indoor swimming pool and sauna, a nightclub and discotheque, an art gallery and a pretty 8-hole golf course. The links are meticulously and harmoniously laid out on 200 acres (80 hectares) of hilly terrain between oaks and lime-trees. Hotel guests naturally receive a discount on the day ticket.

To take one of the riding courses (all levels) would require an extended stay in Lipica, but while you are here there is always time for a ride out or a spin in a carriage or, for that matter, for a guided tour of the farm. The pony-rides are extremely popular with children. The culmination of any visit here, however, takes place at 11am or 2.30pm: the dressage exhibition with music in the large riding hall. The ease and elegance with which these wiry animals execute their complicated dancing figures is astounding. There are international competitions held in Lipica annually: eg, the Volvo Cup in May, 1990 and the European Dressage Riding Championship in September, 1991.

The Lippizaner stud farm

At the **Hotel Maestoso** you can dine *à la carte*; for those in a rush there is also a pizzeria. The hotel reception will be glad to arrange a visit to the nearby caverns in Skocjan and Vilenica.

The most prominent attraction in the northern karst region, however, is the dripstone cave at **Postojna**, also known as the Adelsberg Grotto. A small electric train takes you on the 1½ mile (2.5 kilometre) descent through a bizarre, wonderful world of stalagmites and stalactites,

You have to walk the remaining 3¾ miles (6km) of the tour: across footbridges, up and down stairs and along galleries. But once you begin to feast your eyes on this spectacle, you will agree that it was worth the effort—as skilful lighting picks out scenes of overwhelming beauty: Calvary Hall, the Ballroom, the Gothic Hall and the Crystal Suite shimmer and sparkle in multi-hued splendour.

The subterranean concert hall is 215ft (65m) long and holds an audience of 10,000. Isolated from all aeroplane noise; traffic vibrations and street sounds, its fabulous acoustics bear comparison with those of any cathedral or recording studio. If you are attending one of the occasional concerts or are simply taking part in the tour (which takes a good two hours) I strongly recommend a warm wrap: the temperature in the grotto is a cool 8°C (46°F), and it seems even colder by contrast with the heat of outdoors. After the caves, it is time to return to Pula or drive on to Piran for a cozy dinner.

What distinguishes **Piran** from the many resorts along the Istrian coast is its special charm and the fact that it is not yet dominated by hotel high-rises or holiday villages—and long may this remain so. The main square is dominated by a monument to the violinist and composer Tartini, who was Paganini's teacher. The town wall has fallen into disrepair. The legend about its seven towers says that one should let them speak. Perhaps they were originally meant to speak to prospective conquerers, saying: "Do not dare touch us"—today they seem, rather, to welcome the visitor to the narrow streets around the Venetian palace and the patrician houses of Piran.

Tour 3

A Basilica and Romance

A day trip to Poreč with its St Euphrasius Basilica; by boat through the Lim Fjord; the romantic city of Rovinj.

If you are not travelling by car, you should go down to the Pula coach station in the morning and buy a ticket to **Poreč**. Calculate a little over an hour for the 45-mile (70-kilometre) trip. The departure times vary with the season, so you should check the indicator board under *Polazak* (Departure). You might as well check *Dolazak* (Arrival) while you are at it—then you will know when the last or next-to-the-last bus returns from Rovinj. On the busy main road between Pula and Koper, most long-distance coaches stop when people flag them down: either at bus stops or at the turn-offs to the seaside towns.

The **Istrian Peninsula** is full of variety: the contrast between the narrow fertile valleys with their red earth and lush, green vegetation, on the one hand, and the grey karstic rock formations, on the other, is particularly striking. Even without a car you can reach tiny, barely populated villages in romantic locations—generally on top of hills—along many of the roads. **Vodnjan** (with a branch of the Pula Folklore Museum offering a remarkable collection of religious art) has a few hundred inhabitants; Modovun and Beram likewise; Hum and Roć, Buzet, Draguć and Grožnjan even fewer. These places are reminiscent of the old hilltop towns in Tuscany. So is **Pazin**, a larger town with a population of 4,840.

Hum and **Roć**, in particular, were major centres of ancient Glagolitic literature as early as the beginning of the Middle Ages. To this day, they harbour stone evidence of this ancient culture and its religious history. Hidden in a tiny woods not a quarter of an hour's walk from **Beram**, the humble church of **Sveta Marija na Škrilinah (St Mary on the Stone Tablets)** prides itself on its important frescoes dating back to the 15th century. These remarks should suffice as inspiration for further excursions.

At the moment, however, our primary destination is **Poreć**. Going back to Roman times, the main road, **Decumanus corso**, ends at **Marafor Square**—the ancient Forum. What is left of its stones now supports some of the houses built here. On a walking tour of the town, you cannot miss the Canon House, the House of the Two Saints and Romanesque town house on Marafor Square, any more than you can the two fortified towers, but you will have to search a bit for the entrance to the **Basilica of St Euphrasius** and the Baptistry. As you head down Ljubljanska ulica, the parallel street to the Decumanus, you will find a side alley leading to this most magnificent church building in town. It harbours some wonderful mosaics: some are from older temples and some have been restored. The complex of buildings is one of the few surviving examples of Early Byzantine architecture.

You can book a tour of the city through **Adriatic Travels**, Obala Maršala Tita. And while you are there, you might also ask about the boat tour to the **Limfjord**. The boat runs through the Poreć Lagoons into the fjord and then through the **Limski Canal**, a nature reserve known for its mussel farms. Reaching 8 miles (12km) into the interior, the fjord is a natural habitat for numerous species of fish.

If you are lucky the travel agency will also be offering a coach transfer for the return trip from the Limfjord. This coach occasionally also takes passengers to Rovinj. If this not available, ask for directions for the boat which will take you directly to Rovinj.

You should try, at any rate, to see **Rovinj** before nightfall. After a stroll through this romantic city it's time to head for a good restaurant. There are many around the harbour, but one I especially like is the **Amfora** (A Rismondo 23, Tel: 815525) where I recommend the redfish.

If you look at the top of the tallest church tower in Istria, you will see the symbol of Rovinj: **St Euphemia**, keeping an eye on all the offshore islands as he revolves in the wind. You can visit one of these islands, **Crveni Otok** (Red Island), in the evening—on one of the 'moonlight boats'. When it is time to return to Pula, just follow Beogradska ulica to the coach terminal. In the same street is the septagonal **Baptistry**, going back to the 12th century, and a small but striking Chapel of the Holy Trinity.

In **Vrsar** there is a small airfield noteworthy not only for its competitions and training, but also for the sightseeing flights which can be chartered. Viewing Istria from above is a lovely alternative to a package boat ride and seafood picnic.

Poreč harbour

Tour 4

Brioni: Tracing Tito's Footsteps

An afternoon tracing Tito's footsteps: the tranquil Brionic Islands with a safari park and various museums.

Even the ancient Romans loved the Brionic Islands and established settlements here. In 1893, after changing rule and their creeping deterioration during their affiliation with Venice, an Austrian bought the Islands. Paul Kuppelwieser built hotels and bathing facilities, laid out a golf course and built a race track and tennis courts. Assisted by the bacteriologist, Robert Koch, he renewed the island's infrastructure, laying a waterline from the mainland and building a network of roads, which were supposed to make this paradise attractive to an exclusive elite around the turn of the century. In the 1920s things went downhill for these luxury properties and the war made things even worse. The name Josip Broz Tito is associated with the rebuilding process which began in 1947. The main additions during the early 1950s were the residence on **Vanaga** and the villa on the main island of **Veliki Brioni**.

The major sights include the remains of a once luxurious complex of buildings, a *villa rustica* going back to the 1st century, the ruins of a Byzantine fort, the remains of an early Christian basilica and numerous works by sculptors from various countries. In addition, the island has a fabulous **safari park**, with an abundance of species, perfect for amateur photographers and the producers of TV commercials. Brioni has even more to offer—being not only a national park but also a **national monument**. President Tito used to take the famous 'Blue Train' to Pula and then, under escort, continue by car and finally by ship to his island residence. Up until a few years ago the islands were off-limits to visitors—with one major exception: the *Brionic Declaration*, the founding document of the movement of non-aligned nations, was signed here by the presidents of India, Egypt and Yugoslavia (Nehru, Nasser and Tito) in 1956. Today anyone is allowed onto the island.

The tourist agency coaches leave from the Arena in Pula and the public service bus to Fažana stops quite nearby. Naturally you can also drive your own car—perhaps following a visit to the collection of religious art at the parish church of Vodnjan, which is practically on the way: that is, on the road to Poreč, Koper and Trieste.

The island administration in **Fažana** has a monopoly on the touristic exploitation of the Brionic Islands. Tickets for the islands, which include the boat ride and a guided tour, are sold at the landing-stage in Fažana. The tourist bureau in Fažana is in charge of arranging hotel accommodation on the islands and in town, as well as renting out apartments and private rooms. You can also book a tour of the island in Pula, either at your hotel or at one of the numerous travel agencies.

In Fažana you go aboard a small ferryboat, which takes about 20 minutes to the island port—where two Presidential speedboats seem to be sleeping in their berths. Here you climb on one of the tiny island trains—cars pulled by tractors disguised as locomotives. As they chug along, swaying you through the countryside, a voice from the tinny loudspeakers will explain the most interesting points along the way.

Later, there is enough time for the zoo, a small folklore collection—a miniature display of the various ethnic groups of Yugoslavia, with traditional costumes, implements and all kinds of tools—as well as for **two exhibitions** dealing with President Tito. Tito's life and activities on the Brionic Islands are portrayed in 200 photographs: the statesman as a nature-lover, gardener, benefactor of poor children and meeting with important international politicians and celebrities. You can also examine the collection of presents which Tito received from all over the world: a veritable zoo of stuffed exotic animals.

A very refreshing way to spend the time remaining until the boat leaves is to head off for a walk on your own. Also you should not have any trouble finding a driver willing, for a small fee, to take you to the **Kuppelwieser tombs** and to the **villa rustica** (or simply ask for Bonita, the guide). On the main island there are three hotels at your disposal, offering tennis courts and an indoor pool, as well as horseback riding and carriage rides.

Tour 5

To the Roots of Croatia

Worth at least driving through: the islands in Quarnero/Kvarner Bay, Cres, Lošinj and Krk; several routes.

These popular islands lie in Quarnero/Kvarner Bay—between Istria and Dalmatia. For short stays the use of a car—either your own or a rental—is more convenient than resorting to the few bus lines. Arriving from Pula by way of Labin, you board the ferry—connecting Brestiva with Porozina on the island of Cres—at the terminal, a small ramp 2 miles (3km) below the coastal road. Ferry tickets are sold at the kiosk next to the patient queue of waiting cars. The crossing takes about 50 minutes.

On the island, a mountainous road takes you through remote regions to **Cres**, the tranquil main town on the island. The inviting setting includes several pleasant, modest restaurants and an old but renovated hotel by the picturesque harbor. The **Franciscan monastery** with its beautifully carved choir stalls, the old, as well as the new parish church and the **Municipal Museum** in Palais Arsan—with its collection of ancient amphoras and coins—are all worth visiting.

If you are arriving from the direction of Opatija or Rijeka, there is another way to Cres: by first crossing the **Tito Bridge** (requires a toll) at Kraljevica to the largest island in the Adriatic, the **island of Krk**. The main town of the same name is not only

interesting for artistic and historical reasons—mainly the **Cathedral** and the **Quirinus Basilica**—but also enticing for its particularly delicious ice-cream parlours and the pastry shops called *slastičarna*.

On the south side of Krk Island there are two places of vital importance to the Croatians' sense of cultural identity: the former large town of Baška and its suburb, **Jurandvor**. The *Baščanska ploča*, the slab of Baška, is the oldest irrefutably dated document written in the Croatian language and using the Glagolitic alphabet. Today, there is a facsimile of this special national treasure deposited in the wing of the reconstructed altarpiece in the **Lucija Church** in Jurandvor. The original is in the custody of the Yugoslavian Academy of Arts and Sciences in Zagreb.

There is a regular ferry connection between **Valbiska** on Krk and **Merag** on Cres. From the town of Cres I would recommend the road to **Osor**. If you are travelling by car and are in the mood for a small detour, the turnoff to **Valun** will take you along a rather adventurous stretch of road to the hamlet of **Lubenice**, apparently inhabited only by a couple of old women. However, the view way out across the sea from the vantage point of this village, its surprisingly splendid church and the burial chapel in its cemetery make this detour well worth the hour (approximately) it takes. The road to Osor takes you past a natural wonder: **Vransko jezero** or Vrana Lake. 242ft (74m) below sea level at its deepest point, with its surface 42ft (13m) above sea level, this body of water still baffles science. It supplies the cities of the islands of Cres and Lošinj with drinking water and provides travellers with an astounding sight. For hygiene reasons, the water is strictly off-limits.

In ancient times Osor was a major trading centre and is said to once have had a population of 20,000—today it is less than 100. Still, the international music world loves the tiny town for the musical soirées in the summer, largely dedicated to classical and contemporary chamber music. Osor also features an exhibition of sculptures on musical themes. Behind the remains of Roman town walls, (sun)bathing fans will find ample space on the rocks at the edge of the woods, and windsurfers are delighted by the fresh breeze which blows in the bay.

At the far end of the bridge—sometimes opened for small ships—you can see the island of **Lošinj**. In the summer, unfortunately, it is so popular that the roads are always jammed. From **Nerezine**, where there is a traditional fair on the first and second of August, the road continues to the main town, **Mali Lošinj**.

View of Cres

With its picturesque location, the harbour is considered to be one of the most beautiful on the Adriatic. A popular walk (2½ miles/4kms) ends in **Veli Lošinj**, featuring the famous park laid out by the heir apparent, Karl Von Habsburg, containing hundreds of thriving trees from all over the world.

In Mali Lošinj you have your choice of two major ferry connections—depending on whether you want to head back or travel on: the ship to **Pula** takes 3½ hours, whereas to **Zadar** you will need just over 4 hours. In the event that you either decided to see Krk after Cres and Lošinj, or have simply discovered so much on Krk that you have decided to skip the latter two altogether, then I recommend you catch the ferry to **Senj** in Baška.

Situated at the foot of the Velebit Mountains, the city of the brave Uzkoks is certainly no gem. In the cellar of the **Nehaj Fortress** above the city, there is a speciality restaurant, however, which opens its doors in the evenings. Just ask one of the taxi-drivers to drop you there and arrange for him or her to pick you up again at a particular time. You will enjoy the view more if you come back during the daytime—when you can also see the fortress and the municipal museum with their stony relics of heroic days gone by. The island of **Rab**, by the way, can also be reached from the coastal road: by taking the ferry from Jablanac. It is another good 6 miles (9km) from the landing stage at Mišnjak to the City of Rab—and there is no regular bus service. Rab is certainly worth seeing and a very popular resort, especially with visitors from Bavaria, indeed it is said that, in the summer, one can learn German here just by sitting and listening. Reputable restaurants on this route are: the **Simona** in Rijeka, the **Puzev breg** in Opatija, and in Njivice, on Krk Island, the **Rivica.**

Zadar

The city of Zadar is the base for the various excursions described in this section. The city's most attractive features are the rich cultural life and a pleasant climate. Most of the time a gentle breeze blows through the streets, warding off the kind of oven-like temperatures prevailing in many of the more confined old towns.

History

Zadar has had an eventful history. Settled as early as the ninth century BC, and bearing the name Jadera, it developed into a major trade and seafaring centre. The Romans conquered the settlement during the second century BC. The regular network of streets in the fortified Roman town with its three town towers has been preserved to this day. A water main connecting the city with the inland lake, Vransko jezero, 22 miles (35km) away has existed ever since the rule of Emperor Trajan. Even before that the town had thermal baths, a sewage system, a Capitol and an amphitheatre. You can still make out the ancient Forum.

Several years ago an ordinance was passed prohibiting construction without prior inspection of the historical ground—and in the event that finds do turn up, they must be evaluated or recorded first. Scientists assume that the city was shaken by a disastrous earthquake during the sixth century. To the Awares and Slavs arriving here during the seventh century, the old Roman city appeared to lie about a metre lower than the surrounding area. It still remains a mystery whether tremendous tectonic forces raised the ground at this spot, or whether they lowered this spit of land almost to sea level with the entire city on it.

Having fallen under Byzantine rule, Zadar became the seat of the Eastern Roman imperial governor. Later, as Slavic influence prevailed, it became a Glagolitic, or ancient Slavic, diocesan town. It fell upon Zadar to lead the coalition of Croatian cities joining forces against the Venetian claims to power. This fighting lasted a good 400 years, with Zadar being conquered six times up to 1409—when King Ladeslaus of Naples sold all of Dalmatia to Venice. It was also during this turbulent period—in 1202, to be precise—that Zadar was ravaged by impoverished French crusaders.

And yet, after each setback, the city began to flourish again. Croatian-Hungarian kings resided here; Romanesque and Gothic buildings were commissioned. Venice's iron rule lasted from 1409 to 1797. The population was gradually Romanised through immigration, though marriages with the inhabitants of the Slavic hinterland were prohibited. Napoleon's victory remained no more than an episode—causing a brief upturn inspired by the French Revolution. With the help of the British war fleet, however, Austria succeeded in conquering Dalmatia. The Austrians then proceeded to subject the coastal towns to a resolute campaign of Italianisation. Zadar now became the centre of a movement for the rebirth of the Slavic nation, a nationalistic and cultural grouping; poets founded magazines, cultural circles and schools in order to preserve and cultivate the Croatian or Serbo-Croatian language.

However, in spite of the rebirth of a southern Slavic nationalist movement, the area had to suffer Austrian rule until 1918, and Italian occupation until 1943. In the Treaty of Rapallo (1922) it was proposed that the city become part of an Italian enclave on the coast of the new Yugoslavian state, formed by the former kingdoms of Serbia, Croatia and Slovenia. When the fascists took power in Italy, there followed a more repressive period imposing an Italian way of life on the 8,000 inhabitants; half of them, preferring to retreat to the hinterland, were replaced by new settlers moving in from Italy. At the end of World War II the city was totally destroyed by allied bomb attacks. During the period of reconstruction a great number of cultural monuments were restored

Tour 6

Forts, Monasteries and Churches

The historic heart of Zadar with its innumerable sights: churches monasteries, towers and museums; dinner at a seaside fish restaurant.

On your first day in Zadar you will probably discover that the historic heart of the town presents so many fascinating sights that you will want to pay a return visit to several of them: to examine a particular collection more carefully, to revisit a museum or attend a church concert.

If you have just arrived from the motorway, the train station or the coach station, then you set out by walking along the **Jazine Harbour Basin** to your right, keeping the tall wall of the bastion to your left, until you come to the passenger ship landing-stages. As you pass the city gates on your left, you do not cross the pedestrian bridge. If you have just arrived by ship from Rijeka or Pula, or by bus from one of the neighbouring holiday villages, such as Zaton or Nin, Borik or Petrčane, then you are already at the bus terminal or ship landing-stage which is the designated starting point of our tour of the city.

Coming from the **Radniča obala** (Worker's Shore), cast another glance at the defensive wall in the water of the harbour. Remember the spot: you can come back here later and hire a rowing boat to take you across to visit the other side. Next, you pass under the walls of the former city fortification, now supporting a promenade bearing Lenin's name: **Šetalište Vladimira Iljića Ljenina**. In front of the **Pred Arsenalom**, the large arsenal used as a warehouse these days, you turn to the right. There you will see the old **Fort**, with embrasures in its walls, a hexagonal tower and a small arsenal converted into an art gallery. It was from here that the Venetians managed to keep a tight rein on the rebellious populace for quite some time. Hidden behind some trees at the Square of Three Foun-

Benedictine convent, home of the Zadar Gold and Silver collection

tains, **Trg tru bunara**, you will discover the **Church of the Madonna of the Fort**—or, at least, the remains of this church, also known as 'Our Lady of Health', along with an onion-shaped bell-tower. The picture of the Madonna is now located in the Cathedral. Keeping to the left of the tanker shipping administration building and the fenced-in grounds of the customs authority, proceed down Ulica Borisa Kidriča to the Bastions of St Nicola and St Francis. The **Franciscan monastery** and the **Sveti Frane Church** house important works of art. They require an appointment, but are well worth the visit.

Back outside, you pass the Bishop's Palace to discover the outer demarcations of the ancient Roman Capitol: plinths decorated with reliefs, battered by the passage of time. The solitary **pillar** standing in the middle of the forecourt served as monumental stocks during the Middle Ages; the chains on this pillary are said to be the original mediaeval ones. From the edge of the Forum you also have a beautiful view of the offshore island of Ugljan.

The **Forum** is also the location of **St Mary's Church** with the adjoining **Benedictine Convent**. The nunnery was founded by a noblewoman named Čika or Cicca; the first abbess being the half-sister of the Croatian king, Crešimir IV. Remarkably, the Reverend Mother also had a daughter. The Church of Holy Mary was built in 1091 under the direction of the mother, whereas it was Vekenega, the daughter—in the mean time herself promoted to abbess—who commissioned the **belfry** in 1105. In the adjacent convent, the world-famous **Zadar Gold and Silver collection** is laid out in eight showrooms on two floors. Discover for yourself what reliquaries, monstrances and other precious items are waiting to be marvelled at here (open from 9.30am–1pm, 2am–7pm).

Once you have finished feasting your eyes, you again turn to the right, passing the archaeological museum—not created here until 1973 and well worth a visit later. Right now, however, your tour

Zadar market

takes you on past the Church of **Sveti Krševan**, with its still unfinished belfry, to the Harbour Gate. Incorporating parts of a Roman triumphal arch, it bears a plaque commemorating the sea battle of Lepanto. The lion on the outer side demonstrates that Venice reigned here at that time.

The walk back into the centre of town grants you another look at the exterior—especially the apse—of the historically significant Sveti Krševan Church. The relics of the saint with the pre-Slavic name Chrysogonus—one of the city's major patron saints, along with Simeon, Anastasia and Zollus—are preserved here. Continuing along **Sarajevska ulica**, past the palaces of the families Gverini and Fanfagma and past churches dedicated to St Andrew, St Marcella and St Peter, you will reach the **Market**. Its lively hustle and bustle provides a striking contrast to the adjacent ruins of the Church of the Mother of God at the old City Gate and the remains of Cedulini Palace.

If you have not already taken refreshment near the Cathedral, then I suggest you now make a beeline down the Ulica 1 Novembra 1944 to **Narodni trg** (People's Place or Big Square). This is the centre of town. The somewhat over-proportioned City Hall was built in 1936; the former Guard House with its clocktower—added in 1798 under Austrian rule—is Renaissance in style. The City Loggia goes back to the Middle Ages, when it served as a courthouse where contracts were signed and where, in front of its arcades, decrees and council resolutions were read to the public. There are plenty of cafés here, the most bustling being **Under the Clock**, on the terrace by the Square. For lunch or an in-between snack, you can either turn to St Lawrence, after whom the **Café Lovro** is named, or else walk down Omladinska ulica to the **Restaurant Dalmicija** across from St Simon's Church, Sveti Šimun.

By now it must be high time for the siesta so customary here: time to give your tired feet a refreshing break in one of the parks or back at your hotel. Continuing your tour later in the afternoon, you can stop in at the **Café Colona** by the column to have 'one for the road'. Next comes the remains of a Roman city gate—preserved behind fences in a walled-in recess in the ground; then a visit to the **Church of St Simeon**, who is still highly revered here. This patron saint's magnificent **sarcophagus** is located in the main altar. This great masterpiece, created in 1380–1 by Francesco da Milano in collaboration with two fellow guild members, was fashioned out of 550 pounds (250 kilogrammes) of silver. The two Baroque angels carrying the coffin were added later: they were cast in 1764 using the bronze taken from captured Turkish cannons.

Adjacent to **Trg Oslobodjenja**, 'Liberation Square' with its Roman column, there are several interesting palaces partly housing medical facilities, a library and a modern gallery. In one part of the square, above a cistern, there are the five wells to which the square owes its older name, **Trg pet bunara**. Here, at the foot of the five-cornered **High Tower**, you will find remains of the 13th-century city wall.

Before the cistern and the wells were installed here in 1574, the city was divided from the mainland, first by a defensive moat, then by a navigable canal. The five-cornered bastion goes back to those days and is a **Children's Park** today. The fortification jutting out even further, with its abandoned casemates, is a beautiful, shady park bearing the name of the poet Vladimir Nazor.

Of all the city gates the most beautiful is the **Porta Terraferme**, the Earth Gate: **kopna vrata**. It is located in the extension of the **Ulica žrtava fašizma**, the Street of the Victims of Fascism—where St Michael's Church with its Gothic façade, the Nassis Palace and the large Church of St Dominic—today housing a well-known puppet theatre—are all worth seeing. The outer side of the Earth Gate portrays the patron saint Chrysogonus, riding tall in the saddle, Sveti Krševan na konju and, of course, the Lion of St Mark's from the Serenissima in Venice. The drawbridge over Faša Canal disappeared long ago, but a small boat harbour still bears this name, as does a highly recommendable **fish restaurant** by the waterside.

So, I suggest you descend the steps and reserve a table for the evening, before strolling under the city fortification to the broad shore promenade, past the impressive House of the Philosophical Faculty—below the open-air cinema atop the bastion. The view out over the open sea to the islands is

beautiful—particularly in the light of the evening sun, when the colours begin to glow again. Near the ruins of a church named Stomorica and dedicated to Saint Ursula, there are still a few little crooked streets with traditional restaurants and witty boutiques. Before you start getting ready for dinner, for a concert or a discotheque, why not spend a few minutes on the terrace of the large **Hotel Zagreb**, doing a bit of planning for tomorrow. The 'Rome of Dalmatia', the city of the many churches, has many curiosities to offer, such as gargoyles fashioned after household pets or pre-Christian safety pins.

Obvious places to visit outside Zadar would be the islands in the **Cornati Archipelago** and the resorts along the coast between here and **Biograde;** there are many roads leading to interesting destinations: to the **Velebit Mountains**, to **Pag Island** or the old **lagooon town of Nin**, to **Plitwitz Lakes National Park**. Zadar is an important port with connections to all the major Adriatic harbours and with regular ferry lines plying the waters of the island world that lies off the Northern Coast.

Accommodation

TURISTHOTEL
Tel: 24255
(for the very pretty Hotel Pinija in Petrčane)

HOTEL BARBARA
Tel: 24299

HOTEL NOVI PARK
Tel: 22177

HOTEL DONAT
Tel: 430577

ZATON TOURIST VILLAGE
Tel: 057-64444, 64554, 64123

Restaurants

STARI GRAD
Sime Matavulja 8, Zadar
Tel: 057-441671

Stipe
Dimitrija Tucovića 5, Zadar
Tel: 057-433212

Café Bar Sax
Krešimirova obala 4, Zadar
35 types of wine.
Tel: 057-443570

Niagare Restaurant
Benkovačka bb, Zadar
Tel: 433216

Odmor Restaurant
Jadranska 95, Zadar
Tel: 057-432808

Marko Polo
Koruška 24, Zadar
Tel: 057-23567

Galija
Oktobarske revolucije 23, Zadar
Tel: 057-443553

Bambi
Put Dikla 64, Zadar
Tel: 057-443079

Caskin Laguna Loža
Tel: 051-896426

Miscellaneous

Tourist Organization Liburnija
Omladinska 1
May–October: 7am–9pm
October–May: 7am–12pm, 5–7pm. Tel: 057-22047

Tourist Association
P Cingrije 5
Tel: 057-25948/25040

Sunturist Zadar
Branimirova obala 9
Tel: 33633/22146
Narodni trg 2
Tel: 33633/22146

Atlas
Branimirova obala 2
Tel: 23339

Kompas
Ive Lola Ribara 1a
Tel: 33380

Rent-a-car
Zadar, J Kopitara 1
Tel: 33888

Hotel Liburnija
Tel: 051-896428

Hotel Loža
(with a private accommodation service)
Tel: 051-896313

Kompas
(with a private accommodation service)
Tel: 051-896304

Pag Island

Tour 7

Plitwitz Lakes: Pure Nature

Beyond the mountains, woods and waterfalls, a natural monument of international significance: the Plitwitz Lakes, a magnificent natural setting.

Hidden behind the mighty Velebit Massif—the mountains from which the dreaded easterly winds come rushing down in the autumn and winter—and adjacent to another mountain range, the Kapela, the Plitwitz Lakes were caused by the slow build-up of a karstic river into a series of pools. Once you leave the Adriatic Magistral at Senj, you follow the numerous turns of the **Vratnik Pass**, with its beautiful views into the upland—past a sign announcing the botanical garden nestled between the highest peaks in this range. Then you come to a fork in the road, with the northern route leading to the regional capital of Zagreb. Turning south, on the other hand, will take you to the Plitwitz lakes—here called **Plitvička jezera**. The string of lakes—listed in the UNESCO catalogue of national monuments of international standing—is part of a charming national park.

In the midst of lush mountain forests, the sixteen lakes are connected by waterfalls. Dropping from an elevation of 2,086ft (636m) to 1,575ft (480m) above sea level, the rushing course of the clear mountain water takes it from the bright landscape of the twelve upper lakes to the dramatic cataracts at the lower four. The entire area is criss-crossed by hiking paths; bridges and log roads meander through dense vegetation where dragonflies and the rippling waters seem to try to outsparkle each other.

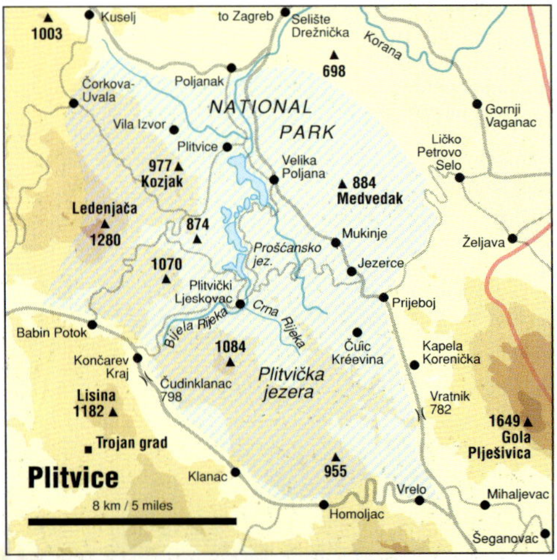

A tour on the sightseeing trains, with their fat rubber tyres, as well as the use of the electric motorboats on the

the larger lakes, are included in the admission fee—with only rowing boats requiring an extra rental charge. Since you can interrupt your rides at will, you can explore to your hearts' content—limited only by weather, remaining daylight and your own stamina. There are places for picnicking on grassy meadows and for swimming in glass-clear waters, as well as a simple, traditional outdoor grill restaurant. Orientation is easy with well-marked paths and there is a general map printed on your ticket. It is valid for an entire day, and you can leave and return to the reserve as often as you like. With several hotels and a large camping site nearby, you can easily spend several days in this natural reserve—one reason why it is as popular with nature lovers and scientists as well as with tourist groups from near and far.

You can also reach Plitvice National Park by public service bus—several lines between Zagreb and the coastal cities pass through Plitvice and Karlovac. If you stay overnight in **Plitvice**, you can spend the evening by the lakes—without the bustle of tourists—enjoying the rustling of the trees and the (distant) roar of the waterfalls. The first tour groups will not arrive until some time after breakfast the next day—by which time you will have finished your morning walk and be ready for new destinations. By the way, along the main road to Zagreb, look out for peasant women selling tasty, home-made meadow cheese.

Tour 8

The Cornates: Island Hopping

A labyrinth of islands: the Cornates off the coast of Northern Dalmatia; a ship excursion for a first impression.

Even astronauts agree: the sea here is bluer than in other places. Take a sightseeing flight from Zadar and you can confirm this impression from an even lower height: 140 islands, both large and small—some, in fact, mere reefs in the sea and yet hardly harmless as far as navigation is concerned—strewn out over an area of 15 by 10 miles (35 by 15km), as if by some heavenly hand.

Most of these islands are barren stony crags of karstic rock, worn by wind and weather, supporting a sparse vegetation of tough, low plants: grasses, strawflowers and pungent herbs (especially sage). Steep escarpments loom up; huge slabs of rock tilted at alarming angles are evidence of the primal forces which once came to bear here upon the floor of the sea, causing the petrified sediment to drop, buckle, crack open and slide upward. Some fig trees, olive groves, scattered clumps of stone oaks, and thickets of Mediterranean stunted pines manage to survive in isolated, sheltered crannies—but of the 24 square miles ($62km^2$) of total land area of the Cornate Archipelago only a small percentage has been cultivated.

In the dim and distant past, there were some sizeable settlements here: some have sunk into the sea, others have been worn away by century upon century of wind and sun. Today, only a few inhabited towns remain—most of them being fishermen's havens. A few sheltered coves have been developed into marinas; others into bathing coves having the advantage of being far less crowded than the beaches on the mainland. Here, where the few human beings are either temporary guests or hard-working fishermen, various rare butterflies, small rodents and amphibians have found ecological niches. Marine life is particularly abundant, with the many unusual algae, sponges and corals indigenous to the waters between the islands and, of course, there is a rich supply of fish around the Cornates as a whole. The major portion of this island world is a national park.

The Cornates are a veritable paradise for sailors, but

scubadiving, submarine photography and aqualung fishing is prohibited. I have visited the islands several times and, with some friendly help, have always found a place to spend the night. For those visiting the coastal cities of Zadar, Biograde na moru, Šibenik, Murter and Vodice, there is a wide variety of excursions to choose from: all the hotels and travel agencies post the times and prices of tours—usually including a fish picnic.

Murter is an ideal embarcation point for a boat outing, often under the expert guidance of a national park representative. When booking day tours you should make enquiries about the exact itinerary and the qualifications of the guide—if one is included.

This is a precaution against a modern form of piracy: although some so-called guides do, in fact, show you a couple of photogenic islands, the cruise there and back winds up taking most of the day, so you spend most of your time and money consuming the boat's abundant supply of wine in plastic canisters. You may, in the end, have had a jolly cruise, but you will also have left this tremendous, curious island world unexplored on the horizon. One day is really too short for the Cornate Islands, but if you can make full use of it, you will at least have grabbed a handful of the stuff of which the ancient mariners' sagas were made.

Between **Pirovac** and **Vodice** on the Adriatic Magistral there is a turnoff to Murter via Tijesno. Murter is where you will find the national park administration building and the information office. This is also where serious underwater photography buffs can apply for special permits. The facilities for sailboat fans not only include landing places, but also a rental servide through the **ACY** (Adriatic Club of Yugoslavia) in **Jezera** on the island of Murter (Tel: 059-78356, 3315); on **Piškera Island** the Club maintains a sheltered marina with service facilities and a restaurant (Tel: 059-34341); ditto on **Žut Island**, where a **Nautical Academy** also offers courses of all levels for sailors and motorboat captains (Tel: 059-34353).

After spending so much time alone with Mother Nature, you may feel like being a bit more sociable for a while: during the tourist season a varied nightlife can usually be found at the hotels and discotheques in **Vodice**. One overnight address worth recommending is the **A P P House 'Vinko'** (Sutjeska 28, 59211 Vodice, Phone 059-43740).

Tour 9

On the Way to Hell

To the diocesan town of Nin; an excursion to the Island of Pag; into the 'Hell' of Paklenica National Park.

From Zadar there is a road leading via Borik to Nin, past the towns of Punta, with a few hotels, and **Zaton**, with its holiday centre. Although quite large, this site—including bungalows, camping site and a row of shops—is so nicely laid-out and well-kept that is one of the few good examples of tourist development in the region. From a distance the holiday park discotheque looks like a futuristic factory, an impression emphasised by the long rows of lamp posts in the vast parking lot next to it. There is room here for 3,500 dancing guests; the music is pop and rock of top quality—and played at top volume.

Having considered this tip for some coming evening, let us now focus our attention on **Nin**, where the Croatian bishops resided up until the 19th century. Just before reaching the town, you will come to a small **church** on a hill surrounded by fields. Dedicated to Saint Nicholas, its dome was converted into a defensive tower fortified with battlements during the Turkish Wars. Inside the town, you will find the **Church of the Holy Cross**, a well-preserved, but now unused building going back to the 9th century—originally erected as a burial chapel for Prince Godežav. What is remarkable is the arrangement of the windows and the orientation of the ground plan—designed to allow both sunlight and moonlight to enter at certain times of the year, according to the astrological calendar. Remains from Roman times indicate the existence of a Forum, a temple to Diana and even an amphitheatre.

Beyond the lagoon around the city, the flat, elongated island of **Pag** comes into view, while the Velebit Range looms up majestically in the distance. Since some sections of the direct road between Nin and Ražanac are in a very bad state, you should drive back to Zadar and take the road by way of Posedarje, Ražanac and Miletiči to reach Pag Island. In the panoramic view, from the vantage point of the high bridge, the sea resembles a moonscape with water. With bus lines running regularly from Zadar to Zaton, Nin and Pag, you need not necessarily use your own car today. Beyond the town of Gorica, in the middle of this barren island, a distinctive strip of reeds stretches out along the road, indicating an arm of water. Between the reeds and scattered clumps of bushes, small herds of goats find shelter and grazing land. Further along the road it becomes apparent that the body of water is a network of

salt works connected with the sea. Bridges and a system of salt pans and salt stores flank the road as it enters the main town on the island. The Church of the Assumption of the Virgin Mary, the never-completed Bishop's Palace, the Late Gothic Prince's Court or the Rector's Palace, the defensive tower and several town houses, as well as St George's Church at the end of the main street are the major attractions. Sadly, the surrounding countryside has been spoilt by tourist development.

The situation is more serene around the **resort of Novalja**, with its numerous idyllic bathing beaches (also for nudists), several good hotels and nice restaurants. One of them belongs to a regional dialect poet whose name is known well beyond the confines of the village: Boris Palčiš Caskin. Sitting in his place, the **Caskin Laguna Loža**, you have a box-seat view of the seaside promenade. The fish arrives fresh daily, and you can have a look at it before it is prepared. Try the light house wine, *Žutica*, with its yellowish shimmer; the red wine is a slightly rough, but honest beverage—and thus more suitable with meat dishes. Do not forget to try the famous Pag cheese: Paški sir. Like the lamb and goat meat from the island, it not only has the aroma of wild herbs, but you can also taste the salt from the air. The wild winds which come rushing down from the heights of the Velebit, churning up the waters between the mainland and the island, carry salt onto the pastureland. Sometimes you can even taste it on your lips.

If you would like to spend the night in **Novalja**, the **Hotel Laguna** is only a few steps away. The next morning, however, you should make your way to **Stara Novalja** to catch the ferry to **Prizna**. As you head toward Zadar, passing Karlobag with its dreamy landing-stage and the church steeple tilted by an earthquake, you will come to a playground for hardy hikers: the gigantic rocky landscape near **Starigrad**. **Paklenica National Park** gets its name from pitch and hellfire—and it can, in fact, get as 'hot as hell' here. Nonetheless, I still recommend this 'hellish tour': it does not take a four-hour march in scorching heat to get the most out of this mountain world: a natural spectacle bearing comparison to any light show.

Split

Split, the largest city on the Yugoslavian Adriatic Coast, is a centre of trade, sports, culture and tourism. As a major harbour, it is also the head of an axis, rich in tradition, between the hinterland and the Mediterranean. History has left a multitude of marks on this city and the neighbouring towns. Split is where visitors transfer to the popular resort islands of Brač, Hvar and Vis; it is not far from numerous cities worth seeing, such as Šibenik, Trogir and the Kaštelam; and it opens channels to the upland, to the area around the River Cetina.

History

Split and the general area around it have been inhabited by people since the Paleolithic period. As early as prehistoric times, Illyric Dalmations settled in Solin Bay—stretching from the towns called 'kastela' all the way to Trogir. Ancient Salona became a harbour and the most important settlement site. In what is now the city of Split, the insignificant settlement of Aspalathos began to develop. The name, of Greek origin, refers to the Spanish broom still indigenous to all of Dalmatia. The Greeks colonised towns along the coast and on the islands—their oldest settlement, Issa, becoming **Vis**, Pharos turning into Hvar, Korkyra melaina evolving into the name Korčula.

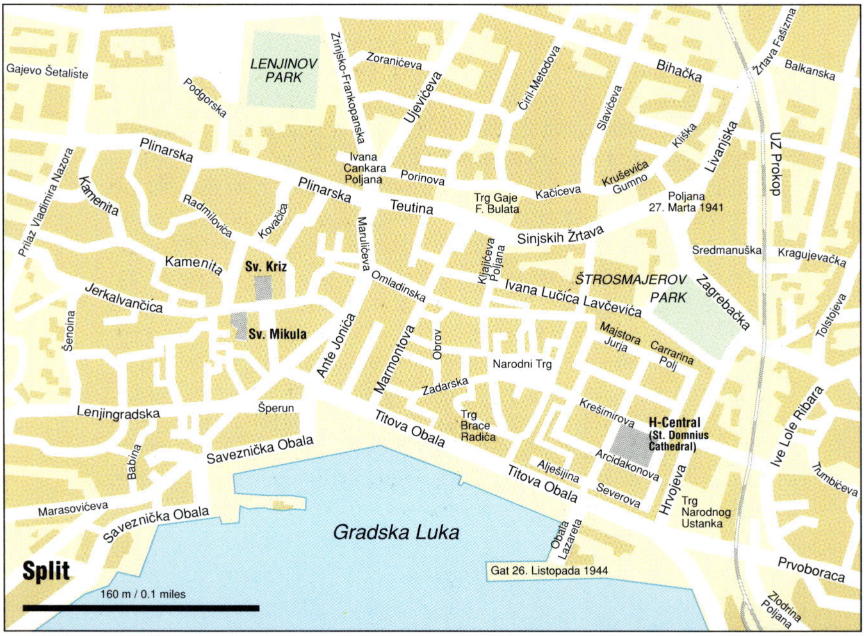

Roman ruins in Split

With the Roman victory over the Dalmatian tribe in 78BC, a temple to Diana was erected on the promontory. Toward the end of the third century, the Emperor Diocletian, himself a native of this area and a bitter enemy of the Christians, had a palace built by the sea which would become the heart of Split.

At the beginning of the seventh century, the Awares entered this area, destroying Salona. The diocesan town was moved from Salona to Split. The church, having gained possession of valuable relics of the Martyrs of Salona, developed into a major centre. In the beginning, Split placed itself under the ecclesiastic rule of Byzantium. During the ninth century, the Croatian state evolved nearby. In Split, the Croatian segment of the population grew steadily—the Slavs mixing with the Romanised population.

In 1075, with papal assistance, King Zvonimir was crowned King of Croatia and Dalmatia and succeeded in gaining control of semi-autonomous, yet still Byzantine, cities such as Zadar, as well as Split.

Split flourished during the some 300 years under the Croatian-Hungarian crown, evolving from a Romance into a Croatian city. In 1420, however, an insatiable Venice conquered Split, ruling here until 1797. The entire 16th and 17th centuries were dominated by defensive battles against the Turks. As a consequence of these two centuries of fighting, Split became a fortified town.

After the overthrow of the Venetians, Split placed itself under Austrian rule which lasted until 1795. The next eight years under the French brought a great deal of modernisation. Napoleon's fall in 1814 restored Austrian rule, which remained in effect here until 1918. During this era, Split witnessed a drawn-out political dispute between those who advocated combining Dalmatian autonomy with a strong orientation toward Italy and the proponents of Pancroatian unification. This union was to be postponed until after the First World War.

Split emerged from World War II like a phoenix rising from the ashes. The first People's Government of a Federated State of Croatia was established by the victorious Communists on 14 April, 1945 in Split. An era of reconstruction began which was to trigger off rapid economic development.

Tour 10

A Roman Emporer's Palace

Harbour and market, Diocletian's Palace and the Peristyle, Cathedral, art and churches, museums, Mount Marjan and more. One day itinerary.

I recommend you begin your day in Split at the municipal harbour. The seaward side of **Diocletian's Palace** is nearly always bustling with activity. The seaside promenade, ie the 'Riva' or **Titova Obaly**, has now been blocked off to traffic—much to the delight of the pedestrians. Large ferries also moor in the spacious basin of this harbour. In front of the harbour captain's office building, you have the berths of the hydrofoils, catamarans and 'gliders', the craft which swarm out on excursions and provide transfer services for hotel guests between the mainland and the islands. The airport buses also terminate here. It is only a few steps to the **train station**, and the picturesque bustle of the Market diagonally opposite is particularly lively during the morning hours.

Cutting across the **Market**—between stands selling fruit, vegetables, flowers, basketware, shoes, clothing, sun hats and souvenirs—and then past the Baroque Monastery of St Dominic you reach the **Silver Gate**. Here, you enter the palace which the Emperor Diocletian had built for his retirement—not quite a regular rectangle and divided crosswise by two streets, which according to Roman tradition were called Cardo and Decumanus. Four gates, double-secured by inner forecourts, led from these main streets out of the Palace. The **Golden Gate** was the most splendid and faced north, toward Salona. The Brass Gate, which used to open directly out onto the sea, was more modest. The Emperor lived on this side and demonstrated the splendour of his residence on the upper floors. The **Iron Gate**, facing toward the west, toward legendary Marjan Hill, is partially hidden by buildings. This is where the first suburb of Split evolved. At the Silver Gate, within the thick walls, various wares are offered for sale: fragrant lavender and rosemary oils in small flasks, traditional crafts, flowers, printed T-shirts and gaudy souvenirs.

The belfry of St Domnius cathedral

The Peristyle

You now reach the intersection of the two axes of the city: the **Peristyle**. This was the cultural centre of the ancient palace; later, in the Middle Ages, the square was used for Christian processions. Running longitudinally along either side is a row of six columns with Corinthian capitals supporting round, beautifully ornamented arches; on the south side the square is enclosed by a tympanum resting on four columns. Sitting in state on his throne in the middle, this is where the god-like emperor received public homage—protected from the adoration of his subjects by an iron grate.

Two Marist chapels were integrated into this part of the enclosure of the square. Above the wide staircase, the middle passageway leads into the vestibule of the Imperial Chambers. Another middle passageway descends into the depths of mighty cellar vaults and out the other side, to the Seashore Promenade. The impressive cellars are marvellously well-preserved. Open to the public, the western cellar rooms are used for art exhibitions and theatre performances, while the underground passage is used by merchants hawking arts and crafts, pictures, earthenware, antiques and extravagant fashion products. I recommend, however, that you save a visit to the pleasantly cool vaulted cellars for the hotter hours of the day. You are still standing in the circular vestibule under the partially preserved high dome. The Imperial Suite to the rear is now an open square overlooking the harbour and the Riva.

Back at the Peristyle, if you take a look at the left or western side, you will see some secular buildings, residential palaces, built later. Incorporated within this ensemble, however, are the remains of a Romanesque town hall and two round temples, today housing a renovated, stylishly old-fashioned **Café-Restaurant**. Radiating modest dignity on the eastern side of the square, you have the small **Church of St Rocco** (Sveti Roko), as well as a 4,000-year-old Egyptian sphinx—whose match you will discover elsewhere a bit later on. The Peristyle is used in the summer for opera perfor-

The bustling market

mances and concerts. When there are no such major events scheduled the busy square is ringed with café tables. Loftily overlooking all of this is the belfry of **St Domnius Cathedral** (Sveti Duje). Dating back to the 13th and 14th centuries, the tower has been altered: in the process of a 19th-century renovation, the Renaissance storeys in the upper section were replaced by neo-Romanesque ones.

The exertion of climbing no less than 200 stairs to the visitors' platform is amply rewarded by a tremendous view of the old town, the harbour and the hinterland. With these comprehensive bearings freshly imprinted in your mind, or with a cup of coffee under your belt and a city map in your pocket, you now enter the **Cathedral**. This octagonal building, surrounded by 24 columns, was once the mausoleum of Emperor Diocletian. The circular inner room of this temple is subdivided into four rectangular and four round niches. Figurative representations have even been preserved from pre-Christian days. You can even discover the Emperor and his wife Prisca here on a **frieze** between the lower and the upper row of columns: portrayed in the midst of merry figures accompanying Eros on the hunt. Don't miss the precious Roman reliefs, the hexagonal pulpit resting on exquisite marble pillars, the choir stalls and the other first-class works of sacred art. Now descend into the crypt, to the **Chapel of St Lucia**, and take a look at the **treasure chamber**; this houses valuable reliquaries, the oldest evangelistary in the city and the eighth-century chronicle of Split's ecclesiastical history. Richly carved by the master artist, Andrija Buvina, the door portrays, amid floral ornamentation, scenes from the life of Christ.

Back outside on the Peristyle, you now cross the square to the west side and enter a narrow alleyway to the **Jupiter Temple**, which has been turned into a Christian baptistry. Here you will also find the second sphynx—waiting for you like a faithful doorman. Next to the font of joined slabs bearing a portrait also representing Christ as King Zvonimir, there are two ancient episcopal sarcophagi and a bronze representing John the Baptist by the sculptor Ivan Meštrović. The portico columns have disappeared, but you can still admire the beautifully ornamented portal leading into the completely preserved *cella* with its unusual coffered barrel vault above smooth inner walls.

You are now ready to leave the temple area, taking the street which is the northern extension of the peristyle, the former Roman *cardo*. Since the beautifully designed **Palais Papalić** is right on your way, you should at least cast a glance inside the inner courtyard. The Palais houses the **Municipal Museum**. The collections of old documents, valuable coins, precious books, furniture and paintings provide ample testimony of Split's history from the 13th to the 16th centuries. If the much-needed renovation work on the museum has been completed, you should make a note of the opening times and continue on your way to the elaborately structured northern town wall.

Facing Salona, the lavishly ornamented Golden Gate looks like a stone puzzle. Still visible, the walkways and battlements give the Gate the appearance of a historical assemblage—including the mediaeval Chapel of St Martin integrated into the structure. In front of the wall, you will find the remains of a Benedictine convent, of a Church of St Euphemia with its adjoining St Arnerius Chapel, and a Baroque belfry, as well as Ivan Meštrović's monumental sculpture of Grgur Ninske, the Bishop Gregory of Nin, who fought adamantly, but in vain, for the introduction of Croatian liturgy. Touching the holy man's foot is said to bring you luck and even to fulfill wishes. The large toe poking out of this pious friend-of-the-people's sandal owes its perpetual shine to the hands of countless adorers. You might as well give it a try; he might just bring you luck.

Diagonally across the way, you can take a breather in **Strossmayer Park**, feeding the pigeons or listening to the splashing of the fountain. The remaining course of the tour follows the palace wall past the neoclassical building of the former municipal hospital—now serving as the Museum of the People's Revolution—to Bosanska ulica, where you turn left. This street takes you to **Narodni trg**, the People's Square in front of the Iron Gate. During the Middle Ages, they built a church into this gate known as 'Our Lady of The Belfry', Gospa od zvonika. the **11th-century belfry**, the oldest in Split, still exists here. The square is surrounded by shops and city palaces in many styles from the 15th century on, with a city café and popular bars in the side streets. Here, you will find an impressive

panorama of urban architectural history. The Gothic town hall going back to the 15th century, in which the first Croatian People's Government was proclaimed after the war, now houses the **Folklore Museum** with traditional costumes, utensils, weapons, jewellery and embroidery from all over Dalmatia. A tour of the collection will show how interwoven the cultural elements of the Mediterranean region were with those from the Dinaric upland.

Next to the museum, you have the Renaissance **Karapić Palace**, and, to the right of the Iron Gate, the Romanesque House of the Cipriano de Ciprianis with a large St Anthony figure in a niche. The loggia of the town guard house and the defiant Romanesque clock building merit particular attention—especially the clock face on the latter with its 24-hour design. When the weather is nice, and on mild evenings, the square is always busy—the café, especially, being a popular meeting place.

Continuing down Marulićeva ulica, you next reach the 'Square of Rebirth', **Trg preporoda**, with its monument to the Split poet born in 1450: Marko Marulić, the 'Father of Croatian literature'—who is considered to be the world's first bestselling author. The original version of his work *De institutione bene vivendi jenes* was published in a total of 15 editions and was translated into five languages. His book *Judita* is considered to be the first authentic work of Croatian literature. The impressive buildings on this square not only include the Baroque **Milesi Palace**, but also the **Venetian Fort** with its well-preserved octagonal tower. This former soldiers' lodgings now houses the **Tower Café** with its open terrace on the tower platform.

According to Mediterranean custom, it is now siesta time. Before returning to your hotel, I recommend a light meal at the **Adriana Restaurant** on the **Place of the Republic**, which you should take a look at anyway. This is the venue for the annual entertainment music festival in July. Or perhaps the luxurious restaurant **Adriatic Club of Yugoslavia** overlooking the ACY Marina yacht harbour may appeal to you more. For truly first-class dining, I recommend the **Opatija Restaurant**, but perhaps it would be better if you reserved a table here for the evening (Pavla Papa 1, Tel: 551921). Whatever your decision, Split holds many more worthwhile sights in store for the afternoon.

Coming from the **Place of the Republic**, you head toward the

ACY Marina to find the **Franciscan monastery** with a church containing the graves of many of the city's most illustrious former citizens. The preserved cloister next to the church represents a harmonious combination of the Romanesque and Gothic styles of architecture. The shoreline drive, Obala Jugoslavenska Narodne Armije ('JNA' is an abbreviation you will see frequently—it stands for 'Yugoslavian People's Army') skirts along the edge of the municipal harbour, and the Šetalište Moše Pijade enters the part of town called **Meje**. This is where you pick up the circular road around the peninsula of **Marjan** rising to a height of 575ft (175m).

Here, the first destination worth visiting is the **Museum of Croatian Archaeological Monuments**. This modern, spacious building provides a good survey of the historical roots of the Croatian people, of the early development of state structures and the founding of the church, of the development of the ancient Croatian alphabet and of typical features of the local style in sculpture and religious architecture. After this, you head on in the same direction, passing the **Villa Meštrović** on your right, surrounded by a well-tended park and garden. **Meštrović** was an important modern Yugoslavian sculptor, and you will come across his art in places other than Split. The villa is where he lived and worked. You should hold on to your ticket, since the price of admission also includes a visit to the **Kaštelet**, a building on the opposite side of the street, housing the artist's large wooden reliefs portraying scenes from Christ's Passion.

Once you are ready to head back into town, you first have to decide which route to take: around Mount Marjan, which takes about an hour; over the top, past the zoo, which can be done in just under two hours; or straight back by bus, which takes a couple of minutes. Perhaps you will see a taxi: in which case you can have the driver take you to the home stadium of the famous football club, Hajduk, at **Poljud**. The athletic facilities are visible from afar, and right next to them you will discover a second, slightly more modest **Franciscan monastery**. There is a unity to the buildings grouped around the simple cloister which gives the whole a particularly picturesque quality.

If you do not wish to spend the evening hours at Poljud Harbour, then stroll on along Zrinsko-Frankopanska ulica, starting at the municipal bath next to the stadium and on past the **Archaeological Museum**, particularly interesting for

The cellar under Diocletian's Palace

its collection of valuable finds relating to the history of Salona. After about ½ a mile (one kilometre), turn left into Teutina ulica to reach the **National Theatre** on Gaje Bulata Square. Perhaps there is an opera or ballet scheduled. The National Theatre is a magnificent specimen of *fin-de-siècle* architecture.

How you spend the rest of the evening is up to you: whether at a play, a concert, cinema or discotheque—or simply over a good dinner with a choice wine. "Those are the nights in Split, with barques bobbing in the harbour..." is how one popular romantic song begins its praise of Dalmatia's largest city. *Laku noč*, good night: under palm trees by the sea.

Accommodation

Hotel Alkar
In the town of Sinj
Tel: 058-82220
Monastery (Museum)
Tel: 82374

Hotel Raskamen
7km south of Omiš
Tel: 058-86157, 86080, 86844

Radmanove Mlinice
outside Omiš; old mill
Tel: 058-96036
Private boat with wine.
Tel: 86344, 86150

Hotel Palace
Kaštel stari
Tel: 058-656022

Hotel Colentum
Murtur
Tel: 059-75255

Agencies

Kornatourist Murter
Tel: 059-75215

Dalmacijaturist
Titova obala 3
Tel: 058-44666
Peristil, Tel: 46472

Atlas
Trg preporoda 7
Tel: 058-43055

Croatia Express
Obala bratstva i jedinstva
Tel: 058-42645

Kvarner Express
Titova obala 17
Tel: 058-42235

Kompas
Titova obala 3
Tel: 058-42993/587280

Turist Biro
Titova obala 12
Tel: 058-42142

Restaurants

Opatija (very good)
Pavla Papa 1, Split
Tel: 551921

Funtana
Renka Šperca 21, 58310 Omiš
Tel: 058-86462

Bife Ivo
58463 Vrboska, Island Hvar

Snack-Bar Fafarinka
Obala oslobodenja 9, Šibenik
Tel: 22-347

Zlatna Ribica
(very good)
Krapljanskih spužvara 46
Šibenik-Brodarica
Tel: 059-72300

Miscellaneous

Tourist Information
Details of the Klapa Festival
(second half of July)
Tel: 058-344

Krka National Park
Šibenik, Andrije Kačića 9
Tel: 059-27720, 27730

Kornati National Park
Murter, Matije Gupca 2
Tel: 059-75058

Tour 11

The Ruins of Salona

Reading stones and seizing the propitious moment: an outing to the ruins of Salona; through the Kaštela towns to Trogir.

For many centuries, Split's access to the hinterland was safeguarded by a fortress visible from afar in the east: the fortress of Klis. Located above Split at the mouth of the River Jadro, on the slopes of the mountain ranges Kozjak and Mosor, lay the historic town of **Salona**. For a walking tour with a visit to the **Museum Tusculum**, you should either get an early start or take advantage of a mild late afternoon and hail a cab for the 3 mile (5km) trip from the centre of town. On the other hand, there are also public bus lines connecting Split with the Kaštelas and Trogir.

In the suburb of Solin, there is a fork in the road, with the upper branch skirting along the parking lot of the excavation site. This is surely the more practical road, because it provides better orientation. The lower, more heavily travelled road passes through further interesting archaeological terrain, as well as an industrial area, leading directly to the theatre of the Forum and to the remains of the once gigantic amphitheatre. I suggest you start at the top, where an orientation sign will help you get your bearings. The excavated sections in the entrance area demonstrate how pre-Christian and Christian periods left their marks in the same place: the later one literally overlying the other. Alongside the road from Split to Solin, by the way, there is a Roman **aquaduct**, which even today still conducts fresh water from the mountains down to Split. And a small parish church on the river island of **Gospin otok**, or Mary's Island, is reminiscent of Jelena, the wife of the 10th-century Croatian king Krešimir II.

The **Kaštela** are a series of seven towns along the cove named after them, Kaštelanski zaljev. These towns owe their origins to 13 fortified castles along the disputed frontier between the Turkish-Ottoman empire and Venetian Dalmatia during the 15th and 16th centuries. These towns are located in the midst of rich vegetation and, although small, their picturesque buildings—worn by the ravages of time—their impressive churches and their hospitable inhabitants have always attracted holiday-makers.

The footpath from the bus stop 'Kaštel Gomilica', via Kaštel Kambelovac, Lukšić, Stari and Novi, and finally to Stafilić is under 2 miles (3km) in length. Since there are always things to see, all along the way, and we may want to rest at one of the small cafés half way there, we should allow a full hour for this inspiring walk. Most of the way, the path passes under trees, past old country seats and the **Hotel Palace** with its magnificent pine park, past bathing spots with children. At the end of the footpath, you need only a couple of minutes to walk up to the road—where you can then wait for the bus to **Trogir.**

Having passed Split Airport, you reach the small island with the town of Trogir. You may already hear its belfries welcoming you across the water. Trogir has an abundance of art treasures. The marvellous **Cathedral**—with its famous portal, the filigree belfry with its beautiful view, the precious cathedral treasure and masterpieces of painting and sculpture—is one of the main attractions. The town hall, the town loggia with the clocktower, patrician houses and the covered fish market, remains of the town fortifications with their towers and gates, are all packed into a very confined space. The municipal museum in **Garagnin Palace**, with its salons and a remarkable library, offers insights into the patrician way of life. There is also a collection of religious art worth seeing in the **Monastery of Saint Nicholas**, a complex network of buildings on the main road. A beautiful relief here portrays the youthful, Greek god Kairos, in lovely motion and with his hair blowing about. The 'god of the propitious moment' seizes something which is hard to grasp. The relief is only a fragment, but as a replica and souvenir it is picked out by numerous tourists in various materials and sizes.

I cannot name a fine restaurant in Trogir, but there is a friendly pizzeria on one of the narrow side streets off the main square, as well as a good tavern a few steps from the Dominican church. A small art gallery at **Šublićeva 17** has a good, convincing collection of paintings, prints and watercolours at affordable prices. Perhaps, having seen them, you will be tempted to take advantage of the 'propitious moment' in Trogir to purchase something which you will enjoy for some time to come. Beyond the bridge to the island of Čiovo, there are several small restaurants and an ACY marina; on the other side of the northern town gate and of the smaller bridge to the mainland, there is a market selling fresh fruit, next to it is the bus station.

Tour 12

The Children's Capital

Worth seeing: the 'Capital City of Children From All Over the World' (June/July); the Krka Waterfalls in the national park.

If you are driving in from Zadar, past Vodice and across the Krka Bridge, the Adriatic Magistral swings around the city centre of Šibenik. If you are driving down from the north, you must follow the signs to Centar. Or you can simply head for the nearly constantly billowing clouds of—supposedly non-toxic—reddish-brown smoke from the Ferrolegura iron and steel works. The bus from the south, or rather from Split (Šibenik lies about halfway between Split and Zadar) takes about an hour. The train ride, on the other hand, is also quite an experience: you travel in a noisy, clattering car, usually with open windows, high above Kaštela Bay and through many a tunnel through the karst.

The train to Drniš, with its peasant market each Thursday, stops in Perkovič. If you are continuing on to Šibenik, you must change here, and it usually takes a good while before the connecting train pulls out. Here I once met a man who sat down in the waiting train, smoked a cigarette with obvious enjoyment, and then headed home to his remote village on foot. That was his own personal way of experiencing the big wide world.

As soon as you arrive in **Šibenik**, I recommend you walk along the **seashore promenade**, hike up **Anna Fortress** Mountain between the tall buildings of the Dolac, circle the mighty walls and enjoy the view of the city and the sea. Up here, in the part of town called Gorica, the cemetery is so cramped that they used to bury the dead standing up—to save space. The crooked, narrow streets of the 'upper town' lead via steps to the Square of the People's Captains, to the Chapel of Saint Krševan, which has been turned into a gallery, and finally to the **Sveti Jakov Cathedral**. The Cathe-

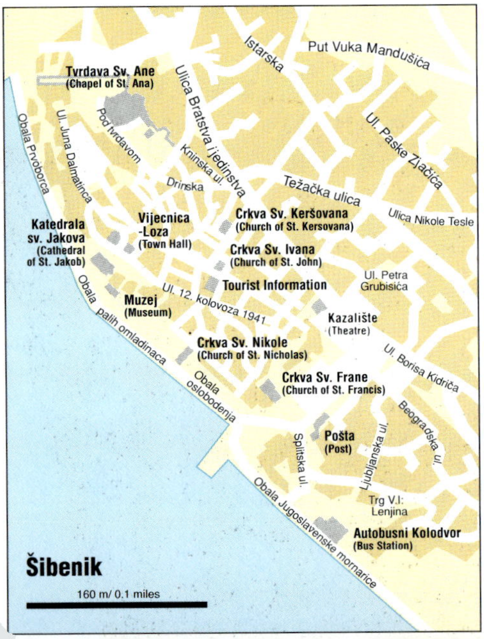

The quay at Šibenik

dral is the most important example of Yugoslavian Renaissance architecture, the principal work of Juraj Dalmatinac, who was held in high esteem, both here and in Venice, as an artist and master builder. The building was begun in the 15th century, but not completed until 1536, using limestone from the area and marble from the Island of Brač. Instead of a belltower, the Cathedral has a characteristic dome with huge tiles arranged in barrel-like shapes. The 74 portraits of contemporaries mounted on the outside of the apse has become the symbol of the city. The side entrance is adorned with the progenitors of the human race, Adam and Eve, in beautiful, naïve nakedness.

Another symbol of this city is new each year and perpetually young: children. Local children, children from all over the country, as well as from the whole world, gather here at the beginning of summer for the Yugoslavian Festival of the Child. They come to enjoy—together with guest artists—plays, dance performances, concerts, puppet shows and movies created for and with children. The guests have included such celebrities as Peter Ustinov and Josephine Baker, Danny Kaye and Sergej Obraszov. For two weeks at the end of July and the beginning of August, the square between the old town hall, with its elegant arcades and the Cathedral, is turned into a large summer stage. The Municipal Theatre (worth seeing), as well as streets and squares such as Medulič and Dobrič, are

also used as performance sites. The Festival features concerts in the Cathedral and the Museum, and there are serenades in the open air. This lovely tradition has existed for over 30 years, since it was first developed under the patronage of Tito. The Festival in Šibenik will probably continue to take place even under the changed political circumstances.

The Rector's Palace with the Municipal Museum, the collection of religious art in the Church of Saint Barbara, the Gothic Church of St John (on the verge of dilapidation) with its beautiful outside staircase, the Orthodox parish church with its precious icons—in fact, the entire, fortunately car-free, town centre entices visitors to simply stroll around at random. Two old fortification systems high above the city, **Sveti Ivan** and **Šubičevac**, amply compensate for the exertion of the difficult climb with a magnificent panoramic view of the sea—and a refreshing breeze perfumed with the fragrance of shadowy conifers. You can also see, at your feet, the

Sveti Jakov Cathedral in Šibenik

harbour of Šibenik and the Krka flowing through a narrow, rock-lined channel into the sea, where the islands actually seem to be floating. Sightseeing boats and ferries, sailboats and motor launches plough through the sheltered bay.

Further upriver, you will find the **waterfalls**. The trip there by water is one option and certainly a charming one, but time-consuming. The other way, by land, is even prettier. After setting out in the direction of Drniš, the road winds its way up the mountains, revealing view after amazing view of the river carved deep into the karstic landscape. Any tourist agency or hotel reception in Šibenik will tell you how to reach the waterfalls in **Krka National Park** or you can take a taxi; it is about 10 miles (15km).

Waterfalls in Krka National Park

Except during very dry summers, the waterfalls are roaring cataracts, magnificently frothing masses of water plunging over limestone barriers. The facilities include a restaurant of the simpler but more efficient sort, all kinds of souvenir vendors and tiny tables selling local products: the sweet wine *prošek*, *lozovača*, a strong brandy, and *Travarica*, a household cure concocted out of spirits and herbs—both tasty and good for, or against, just about anything. Above the waterfalls you will find boatmen waiting for business. You should allow two or even three hours for the tour of the upper course of the **Krka** with plenty of photogenic subjects and a visit to the Franciscan friars with their art treasures on the **Monastery Islands of Visovac**.

If the evenings in Šibenik are fairly quiet (except during festival time), they are all the more turbulent in nearby **Vodice.** For a good dinner, I recommend the **Hotel Jadran** on the seaside promenade or the **Stari Grad Fish Restaurant** on Zlarinski prolaz, only a few steps from the hotel. In the Šubičevac district—I recommend a taxi—the **Uzorita Restaurant** is worth a visit, even late in the evening, for the ample Dalmatian selection of meat and fish dishes and a good wine—accompanied by two gentlemen on guitars.

You will find another family restaurant with a very good reputation in **Brodarica**, a good 2 miles (3km) away in the direction of Split: **Zlatna ribica**, or 'The Little Golden Fish', is a must for anyone with a penchant for all the treats which the sea has to offer the palate, including many different kinds of Adriatic fish, crab, lobster, mussels and many others, all exquisitely prepared and served in a delightful atmosphere of calm and privacy.

TOUR 13

Riders, Singers and Mussels

Equestrian games in Sinj (August); singing contest in Omiš (June); the Franciscan Mussel Museum in Makarska.

The Dalmatian hinterland is an upland region; from the perspective of Split, it lies beyond the tall Velebit and Mosor mountain ranges. The life source of this agricultural area steeped in tradition is the **Cetina**, a gently flowing river, parts of which are very rich in fish. In this region the exchange between the Dinaric and Mediterranean ways of life, and their intermingling over the course of centuries, has resulted in a cultural synthesis.

Here you will still find special and typical examples of local costume and household implements, jewellery and weapons. Whereas the people in the coastal cities and on the islands wear fine scarves, velvet and silk, brocade and lace, the uplanders prefer wool, linen and leather. Within a few generations, however, modern fashions and industrial ready-to-wear clothing have all but destroyed this rich tradition—to the point where only museums and folklore events are able now to convey a hint of that former wealth. The influence of the struggle against and domination by the Turks is still evident, even today, throughout large parts of mainland Yugoslavia, including the Dalmatian hinterland.

Starting in Split, an excursion to Sinj, 20 miles (32km) away, should include a stop at the **Klis Fortress**. Cave lovers should look for a sign along the way, pointing out the **Vranjača Grotto**, which is illuminated and open for walking tours; it contains some really beautiful drip-stone formations. Allow about one hour for this detour.

In Sinj there is a Franciscan Monastery featuring valuable archaeological finds from the Cetina area, documents on the history of the church and the monastery, and a very good folklore collection of traditional costumes, implements, household textiles, furniture, jewellery and weapons. The residential house diagonally opposite the monastery houses the modest

centre of the Knightly Society of Alkars. The large room serving as a museum is dedicated to a special tradition: the *Alka* of Sinj is an equestrian tournament, in which only respectable young men from Sinj may take part. In addition to an impeccable reputation, they need a sharp eye and a strong, sure hand—in order to spear a ring suspended on a string while riding at full gallop down the competition track. This ring—called the *Alka*—has a central hole and three outer fields, so that the hits achieve different scores. The ring tournament is held annually in commemoration of the glorious defence of the city against a superior Turkish force in 1715.

Today the *Sinjska Alka* is a huge popular festival held on one of the first weekends in August. The Alkars, their squires, the honourary princes and the judges are all splendidly decked out and armed; the town is full of flags and music and of guests from near and far. The *Alka* enjoyed great favour on the part of the Serbian Royal Family. Even President Tito honoured this tradition, acting as patron of the contest and donating the challenge trophy: a silver shield of honour bearing his own name on the front and that of the respective champion on the back (now on display at the museum).

On group tours to Sinj and of the Cetina landscape, a rustic lunch is usually followed by a visit to one of the region's folk artists who specialise in naïve sculptor and carvings . The artist presents his works, and the housewife offers guests *fritule*, which are sugar-powdered, deep-fried doughnuts, served up with a robust red wine, while a young man sings ballads, accompanying himself on a *guste* (viola

da gamba) or blowing the bagpipes. This is the sort of encounter you are hardly likely to witness travelling on your own.

It is not far from Split to the mouth of the **Cetina**: 17 miles (27km) along the coastal road in the direction of Dubrovnik. The tiny town of **Omiš** was once a dreaded pirates' hideout along the Amber Road. The daring ruins of forts on the tops and up the sides of the mountains hemming in the city conjure up wild visions of robber barons. The cramped city is full of steps and narrow alleys with tiny shops—offering a large variety of filigree craftsmanship and costume jewellery for sale. The small, bright *Pjaca* is lined with café tables which are always bustling with activity. The **Funtana Restaurant** (Renka Šperca 21, Phone: 058-86462) offers a selection of fresh grilled fish, scampi and mussels of good quality, and the house fish platter is also recommendable.

Omiš is the site of the annual June festival of the Dalmatian *klapa*, a singers' competition lasting several days. A *klapa* is a group of friends singing songs for four voices: songs of love and sorrow, about the sea and tears of farewell, about the joys of life, good wine and loyalty—*sotto voce, a capella*, accompanied by a guitar and a *tamburica*, a sort of mandoline. Traditional songs prevail and new compositions must comply with the conventional style if they are to find favour with the festival's expert jury. During the *Klapa* Festival, Omiš is bursting with people, but also with zest for life and music.

Omiš is also the place where the Cetina forces itself through the Mosor massif into the sea. By car, you can wind your way up the steep turns on the right-hand side of the river, reaching the top of the ravine at the dam wall of the hydro-electric power station. After a glance or two down into the abyss and off into the distance—to the island of Brač, for example—you can head on to visit the villages of the upland.

This area, called **Poljica** after the small fields in the many hollows, looks back on a proud history as an autonomous peasant republic. From the next town, **Gata**—where the local history museum has a lot of material on this subject—our route continues through flourishing gardens and fields, through numerous villages to a small stone bridge at the bottom of the valley.

On the other side, the road continues on from Kostanje via Kučice, partially over stretches of gravel, to Omiš. **Radmanove mlinice** lies on the way, an old mill-fort—today, as a hotel and restaurant, it is a popular destination on country outings—located on the river in the most beautiful, wooded surroundings. It is only 4 miles (6km) from Omiš to here, if you stay on the town side of the bridge and drive up river. A river tour in a small motorboat is an inexpensive and idyllic alternative to taking the car. Just make sure you and the boatman have come to an agreement first about the price and the time to head back to base.

At your destination, the preferred meal consists of trout, fresh from the loudly splashing stone basin in the large, shady garden restaurant. In the hotel it is pleasantly quiet at night, the only sounds being those of the rushing water and a few untiring songbirds. If you are interested and do not mind driving another 19 miles (30km) further south, then why not visit **Makarska** with its unique **Shell Museum** inside the Franciscan monastery. Having systematically expanded the collection since 1959, Father D D Jure Radič can only exhibit about a tenth of the 10,000 or so specimens of mussels, snails and similar sea animals. Another private collection in Makarska shows around 250 different examples of Adriatic fish and sea animals.

From here, you can take the ferry across to **Brač**, a stony island 25 miles (40km) in length. In addition to the famous marble quarries and the **beach of Bol**, Brač has a multitude of places worth discovering. The ferry from **Supetar** takes about an hour to get to Split.

Tour 14

Quiet Coves and Hospitality

An excursion to the islands on the doorstep of the Dalmatian metropolis: Hvar and Brač.

Hvar advertises its sunshine and lavender, Brač its marble and the wandering gravel beach of Bol. There are quiet places and remote coves on both islands. The assistance of local taxi drivers is advantageous, but they are few and far between. Attempting to get some good tips or even personal recommendations from islanders coming over with you on the ferry may present some language problems, but it can also lead to some very pleasant surprises and opportunities for communication, perhaps even resulting in a new friendship or two. The large ferry ships holding lorries, coaches and tourist cars, along with their caravans, are not the only regular connections to the islands. With Split being a major transfer point for package tourists, there are also hydrofoils, hydrogliders and catamarans with roomy cabins shuttling back and forth during the tourist season between Split and the holiday centres on Hvar and Brac; they travel less frequently to Šolta and **Vis**. The latter island is the furthest from the coast and was off-limits to foreigners until 1990. In this sense, then, it is still unspoilt—but also full of prospects for development.

Your island adventure begins in Split, the area in front of the building of the harbour captain, where the airport shuttle buses

Hvar marina

are jammed together. Young people, usually suntanned athletic-looking men, are here representing the agencies. Atlas leads the list ahead of Dalmacijaturist, but this does not mean much. Whenever a transfer boat is not quite full, the resolute individual traveller has a chance to hop aboard—to Starigrad, Jelsa or Hvar on the 'Lavender Island' of the same name, or to Milna, Bol or Supetar on the island of Brač. Wherever you arrive, the drivers of waiting buses or taxis will be glad to help you find a hotel or private accommodation. Also, the agencies and the local hotel company have reception offices in almost every harbour. The magic words are: *turistbiro* and *recepcija*, *Zimmer*, *sobe, camere,* rooms…

In the city of **Hvar** the pieces of architecture worth seeing include the city walls and a fortress, but especially the impressive **Arsenal**, housing one of the oldest municipal theatres in Europe and an art gallery. Also of of interest are **St Stephan's Cathedral** with its cathedral treasure and the **Franciscan monastery**.

In **Starigrad**, 12 miles (20km) away, you can inspect the remains of a Greek cyclopean wall dating from the days when the island was still named Pharos—after the navigational light in operation there. The **Palace** of the Renaissance poet, Petar Hektorović, is a small private fortress also worth seeing. If you care for a swim I recommend the beach in front of the large hotels—from here you can also get a boat to a nudist beach a couple of coves

St Stephan's Cathedral in Hvar

further along the coast where you can relax in absolute peace. The boats going there and back only leave twice a day, though.

If it is total tranquillity you are looking for, then I suggest you first take a ship to **Jelsa**, then a hotel shuttle or a taxi to **Vrboska.** This friendly place, the smallest town on the island, located between wooded hills and a stretch of water, which widens from a mountain stream into a broad sheltered estuary, has a charm all its own. You can climb up onto the roof of the **Church of Holy Mary**—which dates back to the 16th century and at some point was rebuilt into a small defensive fort. Only a few minutes further on, in the **Church of Saint Laurence**, you will find an astounding collection of paintings by Old Masters. Opposite the small island in the middle of town, between shops and cafés, there is a modest, but informative **Fishing Museum**. You can eat either in the **Kozara Restaurant**, or else on the roof terrace of the ACY. If it is already late in the day, however, I recommend the terrace of **Bife Ivo** (58463 Brboska). It is located at the beginning of a pretty, shady walk which will take you to the Hotel Adriatic—just above the Madeira Youth Hotel and the small wharf—in about 15 minutes. Here you can select good Yugoslavian—not just Dalmatian—food from an extensive menu, and the open wine tastes just as good as the more expensive kind in the bottle. As you wait, you can watch the last boats putter into the harbour, by the light of the evening sun, or moor at the ACY Marina on the opposite side.

At the **Hotel Adriatic** you can rent bicycles, boats, surfboards and other sports equipment.

The poet Petar Hektorvič

The next morning, should you either feel a sudden urge to move on to Starigrad or Hvar, or start pining for the car you left behind in Split, or are overcome with curiosity about Brač, the polyglot staff at your hotel reception will be glad to tell you when the taxi boat or hotel shuttle can take you to Jelsa in time for you to make the right connection there.

If you get off in **Bol** and decide you would like to go for a swim on **Zlatni rat**, the 'shifting promontory', you can then climb from there to the **Blaca Monastery**. From Bol several buses leave each day to **Supetar** and **Sumartin**, the two ferry terminals on this island. Taking a car on any of the ferries is not exactly cheap. So, for a brief hop over to one of the islands, you should consider leaving the car behind on the mainland and travelling around on foot or by bus—thus saving yourself not only some money, but also a long wait during the peak holiday season.

In the morning, I recommend a jaunt over to Supetar, from

Starigrad

where you can climb the highest mountain on the island, **Vidova gora**, St Vitus' Mountain, for a grand view. To find the next stop, the mighty **Punta stone quarries** near Pušišća, you need a native to point the way or, even better, a native driver. Most likely he (or she) will also take you to a typical wine tavern somewhere in the interior of the island, before writing down his (or her) address—'just in case' and 'for next year'—and then driving you to catch the last ferry.

Dubrovnik

Dubrovnik is frequently called the Pearl of the Adriatic—and rightfully so. It is no wonder that tourists from all over the world are interested in this unique city, entirely surrounded by its ring of fortifications. Dubrovnik's cultural life, the Summer Festival and the vicinity of a variety of different resort areas, make for an ideal combination. You can explore the narrow streets of the walled-in city at the foot of mighty fortress towers and undertake day tours from Dubrovnik to the city of Marco Polo or to the delta of the Neretva, to remarkable islands off the coast, as well as to places as far away as Montenegro or upriver to the hottest city in Yugoslavia.

History

Refuges and burial mounds in the broad fertile landscape of Konavie, where today the airport is located, verify the existence of prehistoric peoples living along the coast even prior to the founding of the city during the 6th/7th century AD. The rocky island of Lave or Rausa was seperated from the mainland only by a narrow channel and is today the southern section of the Old

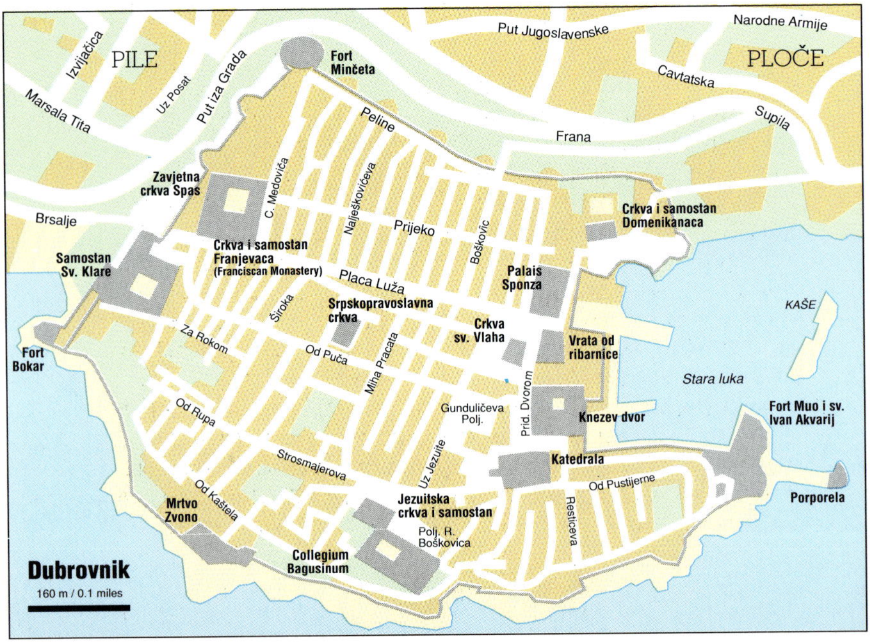

Town. The inlet was filled up later to become Dubrovnik's famous main street, Stradun.

According to one theory, Dubrovnik was founded by Greeks, fleeing here from a neighbouring town to escape the onslaught of the attacking Awares. These refugees gave the new settlement the name Rauzij, which then became Ragus. This genesis, however, was challenged by an important discovery in 1979: during restoration work on the Romanesque Cathedral, remains were discovered of a Byzantine church going back to the 6th century. It is said that Slavs established a settlement not far from Rauzij which they called Dubrovnik, derived from *dubrova* or oak forest.

Dubrovnik/Ragusa grew steadily, but it was also threatened by Arabs, Saracens, Macedonians and Normans. Venice, in particular, had good reason to fear competition from another strong community along the Adriatic. Finally, from 1205 to 1358, they brought their rivals under their control. Despite Venetian supremacy, Dubrovnik remained surprisingly independent—defending its autonomy through clever diplomacy. The city, whose motto to this day is *libertas*, adopted a statute in 1272, which stands out even today as a classic example of a modern constitution.

During the 14th century the city developed into a constitutional aristocracy with a parliament and a government. The ruling governor was subject to strict rules and was only elected for a limited period of time. The purchase of strategically important islands and areas enabled the Republic to become a sea power, while its walls made it practically invincible. The city's increasing wealth brought about the emergence of an affluent middle class and necessitated the development of a comprehensive infrastructure. The Peace of Zadar in 1358 provided the opportunity to break away from Venice. Dubrovnik was able to maintain its position as an independent political entity until the end of the 18th century.

During the 16th century the City Republic owned the third-largest trade fleet in the world, held a monopoly over the salt trade and was an important centre for the manufacture of textiles, metal products and glassware. In 1667 a heavy earthquake wreaked havoc throughout the Republic, and sea trade stagnated, as Europe's major powers refocussed their priorities on the new colonies. Napoleon's defeat in 1806 signalled the approaching demise of the Republic; two years later it was disbanded, with Dubrovnik being annexed by Austrian-ruled Dalmatia. After World War I, Dubrovnik went to the new Yugoslavian state. During World War II, the city was part of the so-called 'Independent State of Croatia', while in actual fact it was subjected to Italian and German occupation until its liberation on 18 October, 1944.

Tour 15

The Pearl of the Adriatic

Surrounded by city walls: gates, towers and a theatre; monasteries, churches and art; an afternoon of siesta and swimming on the island of Lokrum; dinner in town. One day.

I have already mentioned that Dubrovnik is the "Pearl of the Adriatic". As a result, there are droves of 'pearldivers' here: ie tourists from all over the world who populate this unique, fortified old-town ensemble practically the whole year around.

Early in the morning, as the nightly ferries drop anchor in **Port Gruž** and the small market by the harbour is still overflowing, making your way to the busy **Pile City Gate** is still a fairly leisurely affair—you can walk without breaking into a sweat. Strolling past the park high above the sea, past the hospital and the splendid villas with lush gardens, you approach the much-praised jewel. This spot, in front of the largest city gate, the gate leading to the section of town called Pile, is the terminal for many of the routes operated by the municipal bus company, Libertas; this is where the large tour operators have their main offices; it is the starting point for coach excursions and also the taxis stand.

The square next to the street is flanked by a garden café and the elegant **Nautika Club Restaurant**, featuring dancing in the evenings. There is also a fountain for thirsty backpackers. The view of the sea is framed by the **Bokar Fortress**, part of the city fortifications, on the left-hand side, and the rocky height to the right is the main fortification, **Fort Lovrijenac**. It is traditional for the Summer Festival to put on Shakespeare's *Hamlet* here every few years. During the day you can visit the walls. It is said that work began around 1050 on this 160-ft (48-m) high rocky plateau. On the sea side, the fortification is made up of 40-ft (12-m) thick walls; however, those on the city side were designed especially thin. In the event of a mutiny, they could have easily been shot apart.

They say that for a while, there was also a cannon here aimed at the city—just in

Dubrovnik harbour

case the gentlemen of the Grand Council thought of passing resolutions detrimental to the people. Today the only thing shooting here are the tourist cameras and the Fotinbras theatre cannons.

On your first day in Dubrovnik, **Pile** is the name of both your start and your destination. A stone bridge with long benches, built in 1471 by the city master builder and cannonfounder, Paskoje Miličević, takes you outside the city gate. The Stone Gate, going back to 1397, is among the few fragments of walls remaining of Fort Pile—which stood here from 972 to 1818. This entrance to the walled-in, fortified city is completed by the Outer Gate, erected in 1537 in Renaissance style along with the drawbridge across the moat—today used as a playground and park. The statue above the gate is that of the patron saint of Dubrovnik, Sveti Vlaho—elsewhere known as Saint Blase. Go ahead and enter through the first, second and also the third gate—the latter one, Gothic, was erected in 1460 to strengthen the defences of the inner city. Immediately on your left, there is a stairway leading up to the **Town Wall**, nearly 1¼ miles (2km) in length. The total circuit involves some stair-climbing and takes about two hours. In the hot season I would recommend only the early hours of the morning for this tour, or the late afternoon—but the countless pretty views are worth the effort. By the way, since there are three other entrances through the city wall, you can also enjoy the city panorama while walking along individual sections of the wall.

Today, however, let's stay

Island off Dubrovnik

on the ground. The ground right in front of you—the **Placa**, or '**Stradun**' as the people on the street call it—used to be a marshy inlet. Then the Slavs and Romanised Greeks filled it up, so it would no longer interfere with their fraternisation. Today, the Stradun, or Placa, is the main artery, meeting place and urban promenade; this is where you find the shops and cafés, travel agencies and photographers, and much more.

The **Large Onofrio Fountain**, going back to 1438, bears the name of its builder, Onofrio de la Cava, and constitutes the end of the still-functioning water main from the karstic mountains. After the disastrous earthquake of April 6th, 1667—resulting in the loss of 5,000 lives including half the Senate and all the clergy—the destroyed upper portion of the fountain was capped with a dome.

The large building complex to your right is the former convent of St Clare, dating back to the 13th century. This used to be a home for foundlings and orphans and for girls who lacked a sufficient dowry for a marriage befitting their social rank. Today, the large courtyard surrounded by arcades is occupied by a restaurant with musical entertainment in the evenings. Immediately to the left of the Stradun, you will see the Church of the Holy Redeemer, **Sveti Spas**, one of the few buildings left intact after the earthquake. Chamber music concerts are held regularly in the high inner room.

The adjacent **Franciscan monastery** is rich in treasures. Its church tower marks one end of the main street, the municipal bell-tower the other. The cloister has Romanesque columns with richly varied capitals and a well surrounded by splendid, lush vegetation; the setting has a magic all its own which is sure to charm you. The monastery has an extensive library, as well as the third-oldest pharmacy in the world, with a full collection of pharmaceutical implements and all sorts of preparations and scientific literature. Since its foundation in 1317 until today, this pharmacy has performed its services in this same room, though the stylish furnishings and inventory dates from the 19th century. Destroyed by the earthquake, the only thing left standing of the Franciscan church besides a pulpit and a few grave slabs is the *pietà* above the main portal: a stone representation of the Virgin mourning over the body of Christ.

After the earthquake, the city was rebuilt in compliance with new building regulations. This is equally visible in the main street, and the regular layout of the side streets, as it is in the harmonious façades and the shop entrances with their round arches and knee windows. Because of the danger of fires, kitchens had to be installed on the top floor. If you are looking for interesting photographic subjects, just head up any of the alleyways and steps on the left-hand side. Cafés and restaurants, boutiques and workshops all compete for the custom of passing clients.

Continue along the narrow street **od Sigurata** and the parallel street above the Stradun, **Prijeko**. Many of the houses reflect the wealth of their builders. Take a look at the vine winding its way up the façade to the top story of **house number 22–24**—its age is estimated at 250 years. Today, this street forms the narrow restaurant boulevard. Unfortunately, the prices charged do not always correspond to the quality of the dishes. I suggest you resist the inviting posters and menu boards, ignore the friendly words of the restaurant touts for the time being and plunge back into the throng.

The first stretch along **Židovska ulica**, or Jewish Street, takes you through the former ghetto. The adjoining square is dominated by the symbol of open markets, Sir Roland with the Sword. There are just about as many pigeons fluttering about here as on St Mark's Square in Venice. **Sveti Vlaho**, the Baroque church here, is dedicated to the patron saint of the city, Saint Blase. You will find the saint himself, or rather his silver figure, inside the church—holding a model of the city as it existed before the terrible earthquake and the subsequent great fire of 1706. The **Clocktower Loge**, the municipal **Clocktower** and the **Main Guardhouse** make up the east side of the square.

The impressive building along the north side is the **Sponza Palace**, which in the past served as the mint and the customs authority as well as the bureau of weights, the state bank and even a grain warehouse. Today it houses the municipal archives, while the inner courtyard is used for art exhibitions. It also houses the bronze casts of the clappers of the tower bells and the old clock mechanism. Once, in a historical quarrel with the Turkish rulers of the hinterland, the Turks demanded that a sign of their power be mounted at the highest point in the city. The Dubrovnikites assented and an Ottoman column was erected on the roof of this palace. And there it stands to this day—practically unnoticed.

This part of the square is called **Luža**; its extension to the south is called *prid dvorom*, or 'in front of the palace'. The building referred to is the Rectors' Palace, the seat where the rectors spent their one-month terms in seclusion, managing the affairs of the community. In a niche of the Main Guardhouse, by the way, you will discover the Small Onofrio Fountain, a gem of stonemasonry. The building between the Rectors' Palace and the Main Guardhouse is the **Town Hall**. Built during the last century, it now houses the City Café, as well as the lovely **Marin-Držič Theatre**. This complex, open to the town square and to the old harbour, was rebuilt recently, and a cinema was installed in the process.

The Rectors' Palace, built in Renaissance style, is one of the most beautiful buildings in the city. The courtyard with its arcades is the preferred site of the festive concerts during the 'Dubrovnik Summer' festival. The Municipal Museum occupies the top floors; allow a good hour for the paintings and furniture, documents and maps, as well as cultural products of all kinds. You definitely will not have time for the 90,000 books stored here, but you should be able to squeeze in a look at the monument in the inner courtyard. During the era of constitutional aristocracy it was forbidden to erect personal monuments. The man honoured here, however, Miho Pracat, was such a generous donor to his city that this bust was authorised. After all, in 1637, the Rectors' Palace was not yet open to the public. In later years the city's important poets, Marin Držić and Ivan Gundulić, also received monuments of their own—the latter, in fact, in the middle of the marketplace bearing his name.

In the heart of Dubrovnic

The Rector's Palace

As we look around the inside of the **Cathedral**, the most remarkable feature is the winged altarpiece by Titian representing the Assumption of the Virgin Mary. Before the great earthquake this was the site of a tremendous Romanesque basilica—with even older church foundations lying beneath it. A legend associated with the Cathedral involves Richard I, 'Coeur de Lion'. He is said to have found refuge on the island of Lokrum after his ship was smashed to pieces in a storm. He swore to build a church on the site of his deliverance. The island, however, already had a church. On the other hand, the city was pursuing the construction of a cathedral but in need of funds, so they pursuaded Richard to make a significant contribution. There is not sufficient space to list all the Masters whose paintings are displayed in this cathedral, or the overwhelming treasures of gold, silver and jewels, produced by local, Byzantine, Austrian and Italian master craftsmen.

After feasting your eyes, try and find a table in one of the restaurants on **Gundulić Square** or on **ulica od Puča** where I suggest you fortify yourself with mussels or a Dalmatian *pržolica*, a roast meat speciality. Then stroll at random along a few narrow streets, or follow the signs discreetly directing the way to the *od rope* Museum. This 'Museum of Holes' has been closed for quite some time due to extensive renovations. The holes in question are huge grain silos hewn out of the rock. One day the building is intended to house a rich collection portraying the folklore of Dubrovnik and the entire surrounding region.

From the Museum of Holes follow Štroćmajerova ulica past the municipal music school and the mighty Jesuit church on trg Rudera Boškovića, through the crooked alleys of Pustierna, a section of town which still has not been completely rebuilt after the last earthquake. In St John's Fort, **Sveti Ivan**, you can explore the very interesting Navigation Museum with its ship models, sea maps, paintings, treaties and maritime implements of all kinds.

For the afternoon, I recommend a siesta on the **island of Lokrum**. Just take one of the motorships leaving regularly from the Old Harbour, which you reach by passing through either the City Café or the passageway under the Clocktower. Within half an hour you will be on the favourite island of the Austrian Archduke Maximilian Ferdinand—later to meet a tragic end as Emperor Maximilian of Mexico. The island offers the extensive remains of a Benedictine monastery, a botanical garden in a rather neglected state and—the island's main attraction—a nudist beach. Even clothed visitors, however, will find a spot here for a refreshing swim.

Upon returning to Dubrovnik, turn right in front of the Clocktower to the part of town called Ploče. The winding street will take you to the **Monastery of the Dominicans**, which draws many visitors, especially to its church which functions as a concert hall. Near the monastery you will find any number of churches which have either been put to other uses or closed. Heading through **Ploče Town Gate** and past Fort Revelin—used as a summer theatre and for large folklore events—you reach a car park; cross it and descend some steps to the valley station of the cable railway. Treat yourself to a ride to the top of the **Srdj**, or Serge Mountain. The view of the town from here is unbeatable. Lying at your feet in the evening light, the city looks like a toy, a mediaeval miniature. The restaurant on the observation platform has a modest bar; the fortress goes back to the days of Napoleon and, after a brief reincarnation as a discotheque, has fallen back into a deep slumber.

Accommodation

For a long list of high-quality hotels, see *Informator*, a widely available publication which is free of charge.

Four Star

CROATIA
Cavtat
Tel: 050-88022

DUBROVNIK PRESIDENT
Dubrava-Babin Kuk
Tel: 050-22999

Three Star

ALBATROS
Cavtat. Tel: 050-84044

ARGENTINA
Frane Supila 24
Tel: 050-23859

DUBROVNIK PALACE
Massarykov put 20
Tel: 050-28555

EXCELSIOR
Frane Supila
Tel: 050-23566

Imperial
M Simoni 2
Tel: 050-23688

Kompas
I L Ribara 50
Tel: 050-23766

Libertas
Lavčevićeva 1
Tel: 050-27444

Park
I L Ribara 9
Tel: 050-25644

Vila Dubrovnik
V Bukovca
Tel: 050-22933

Hotel Neretva
Mostar, Trg Republike
Tel: 088-24675

Hotel Island Sveti Stefan
Tel: 086-41333/41411

Villa Aurora
Trsteno
Tel: 050-751099

Restaurants

Amfora
Gruška obala 22
Tel: 050-22919

Fish-restaurant Ankora
Ul. Šikora 1
Tel: 050-27589

Mimoza
Put M Tita 27
Tel: 050-26559

Orsan
Zaton (outside Dubrovnik)
Tel: 89267

Koruna
Ston
Tel: 754017

Muta
Počitelj
Tel: 088-800312

Bastiana
Cavtat, Tiha 9
Tel: 050-78312

Agencies

In Dubrovnik there are 26 travel agencies—nearly one on every street corner. *Atlas* has the most bureau offices.

Tourist Information
Poljana Miličevićeva 1
Tel: 050-26302
Information centre
Tel: 26355

Atlas
Pile 1
Tel: 050-27333
Gruž (harbour office)
Tel: 050-33598
Airport office
Tel: 050-77383

Dalmacijaturist
Zrinsko-Francopanska bb
Tel: 050-25890
Gruška obala (harbour)
Tel: 050-24078

Tourist Association Čaplina
Tel: 088-80123

Tourist Association Počitelj
Tel: 088-283

Unis Turist Mostar
Trg Republike 3
Tel: 088-22429

TOUR 16

Plane Trees and Salt Gardens

The rare trees of Trsteno; the mussel beds and salt gardens of Ston; the island of Korčula.

This itinerary takes a full day, but you may choose to undertake only parts of it. Starting early in the morning you can take a country bus from Dubrovnik to Korčula, then carry on to Ston in the afternoon, returning to Dubrovnik in the evening. As an alternative you can make one of the legs of the trip by boat. Someone will be glad to assist you at the **Atlas Travel Office** in front of the Pile Gate.

From **Gruž Harbour** in Dubrovnik, you set a northerly course past the **Bay of Dubrovačka rijeka**—reaching deep into the mainland and once part of the estuary of the Karst river, Ombla; past old palaces, often used as warehouses or garages today; past the lovely yachting facilities of the **Dubrovnik Marina** and through the towns of Zaton mali and Zaton veliki. After about 12 miles (20km) you reach **Trsteno**. At the roadside you will notice two huge, ancient plane trees. Further down the hill you will find the **Arboretum**, a botanical garden laid out in 1502 and featuring an extensive collection of rare trees. The grounds are easy to reach by country bus, which stops wherever you request to get off. The winding paths, an aquaduct and an artistically designed grotto with fountain never fail to delight visitors. Botanists and lovers of horticulture alike are delighted by this place and everyone can enjoy the shade, the fragrance of blossoms and the view out across the sea, all the way to the Elaphite Islands. If you want to stay here, I recommend the **Aurora Hotel & Restaurant** (Tel: 050-751099).

The excursion, however, continues to **Ston**, the fortified town at the base of the Pelješac Peninsula. Still in operation today, the salt gardens were once responsible for two thirds of the income of the Republic of Ragusa/Dubrovnik. As protection against envious and greedy enemies, a wall was built around the city: 3½ miles (5.5km) long and equipped with 40 defensive towers and seven bastions. For protection, the inhabitants of the surrounding villages had to

flee inside the walls. Running up and down slopes, the fortification, even today, is reminiscent of the Great Wall of China.

Ston was laid out according to a plan similar to that used in Dubrovnik. fourteenth-century palaces, the monastery and fortifications will give you an idea of how important this town was to the Republic of Dubrovnik. At the modest hotel in Ston, they will be glad to serve a small refreshment—either Dalmatian ham or the Ston speciality, mussels. In **Mali Ston**, the smaller part of the town, you can order brown *prstace* fresh out of the water, so to speak; the mussel beds lie directly on the 'doorsteps' of the large round watchtower and the old-established **Koruna Restaurant**. The bayside **Kapetanova kuča Restaurant** is also recommendable and, what is more, they have a selection of choice wines—among them, of course, *Postup* and *Dingač* from Pelješac and *Korčulansko blato* from Korčula Island.

The ferry taking you to Korkyra melaina sails from **Orebić**, calling at **Korčula**, which has a wealth of art treasures in the episcopal collection, in the Municipal Museum and in St Mark's Cathedral. Local tour guides, preferably female, take the helm here—with wit, factual knowledge and polyglot capabilities. *Moreška* is held in the spring and summer: a dance spectacle, in which black and red kings fight over a girl. The girl symbolises Christian innocence and the island itself; the kings, battling with sticks, portray Turks, Arabs and Saracens.

If you are to return to Dubrovnik by car I would like to recommend an excellent—in fact, a prize-winning—restaurant. Just before reaching Dubrovnik turn right after Zaton Mali and you will find it, located inconspicuously between the road and the water and called **Orsan**. It is worth a detour, and justifies a night-time taxi-ride from your hotel. You can rely on the owner's menu suggestions: eg: black risotto as appetizer, then scampi, followed by a fish in oil and herbs with a fragrance that I promise you will never forget.

Tour 17

Roman Villas and Troy

A slice of the Orient along the Neretva: Počitelj and Mostar, with fruits, vegetables and fragments of an ancient Ottoman heritage.

The Adriatic Magistral crosses the broad river delta of the **Neretva** near Kardeljevo **Ploče**. This is the terminal of the train line from Sarajevo and the ferry terminal to the Pelješac Peninsula. Here, the Republic of Bosnia-Herzegovena has its access to the Adriatic, after stretching peacefully through Croatia.

For those coming from Split and Makarska, the first treat on the land side is the **Bačinska jezera**, a chain of freshwater lakes surrounded by belts of rushes and clumps of white poplars—ideal paddling territory, with easy access from a nearby camp site. Approaching from the south, on the other hand, from Dubrovnik and Ston, you will find lying at your feet a fertile lowland of river estuaries with ponds and waterways, framed by mountain chains, like a huge garden sloping into the sea.

The road into the interior is lined with colourful farmers' stalls: mountains of melons, hosed down to keep them cool, all kinds of mysterious bottles containing brandies and liqueurs—made from pears, apples, grapes and walnuts—red wine and sweet *prošek* and crates heaped with peaches, plums, apples, tomatoes, cucumbers, eggplants and courgettes.

You leave the road to Mostar and cross the bridge to **Čabljina**, drive past the hotel and all the way through town until the street ends at the bus terminal, where you then turn left. As soon as you see an old steam engine rusting away on the left side of the road and a rather humble tavern on the right, you know you have reached an impressive excavation site: a Roman *villa rustica.*

Gabela, another few kilometres down the road, is where the Mexican author Robert Salinas Price pinpointed what he believes to be the site of ancient Troy. Assessing the geographic surroundings, he identified the Neretva as the historic Skamander River. Whereas his book, *Homer's Blind*

Stone bridge in Mostar

Audience, published in 1985, caused quite a stir in Yugoslavia, the scientific community simply smiled—unconvinced to this day that this is where the events of the *Iliad* took place. After our brief look at this archaeological by-road, it is time to get back on the main track, heading inland.

Shortly you will reach a town girded by fortifications. **Počitelj** was a frontier town in the days of the Ottoman Empire. The old inn and the bathhouse serve as a café-restaurant and as a duty-free shop. The Turkish houses built high up on the slopes have a strange and fascinating aura; some are in a bad state of disrepair. One well-preserved complex has become the home of an artists' colony. Painters and sculptors from all over the world work here; the adjoining public gallery offers impressive evidence of this fact. The **mosque** is open whenever the imam is around and has time, but the **Muta Restaurant** next door is open most of the time—serving typical Herzegovena dishes unquestionably based on original Turkish recipes, as well as plain Dalmatian fare.

Mostar is considered to be the hottest city in Yugoslavia. Its stone bridge is world-famous not only because it is so photogenic, but also because of the local lads who like to prove their courage by diving off it into the waters of the Neretva below. The adjacent Craftsmen's Alley produces copper cans and leathergoods for the tourist trade.

The mosques and Turkish cemeteries are visible evidence that, for a long time, ancient Turkey was a major European power. As offered by all the travel agencies on the Coast, excursions to Mostar include a tour of a Turkish house, as well as a visit to the Karadjoz Beg Mosque. Twenty five of the town's mosques have been preserved; five are used regularly for religious services. Like the mosques, the old Orthodox church in Mostar has a separate gallery for women. Hotels here are generally cheaper than elsewhere along the coast.

Tour 18

In the Land of the Black Mountains

Konavle, Dubrovnik's vineyard and granary; into the Land of the Black Mountains: Montenegro; Kotor Bay; Budva and tracing the tracks of Njegoš.

For a trip to the south you can tour the fertile **Konavle** plateau, around Čilipi Airport, on your own by car. The organised excursions, however, offer at least one additional treat: the programme includes a visit to a naïve painter, as well as to a traditional farm, where wine and dried figs, brandy and plain country cooking are served, while young men deliver their renditions of native and international songs.

On summer Sundays in **Čilipi** at least 40 or 50 coach loads of tourists arrive in the village: to attend mass in the church, take part in the wine-sampling, visit the folklore museum and browse around the market featuring embroidery and souvenirs. The culmination is a performance of regional dance in the costumes of the area. Even the waitresses in the traditional restaurant, **Konavski dvor**—on a millstream a bit off the road to **Herceg Novi**—wear local costumes.

If you were to travel just beyond the area described here, you would enter the Land of the Black Mountains. **Crna gora**, or **Montenegro,** is the smallest but proudest republic in the Yugoslavian

Federation and, since the Congress of Berlin in 1878, a defiantly independent 'subject of international law'. The first place of significance along the way is **Herceg Novi**, the gateway to Kotor Bay. In this area, the mimosas (actually, white acacias) are already in blossom in January. Here, the Oriental influence becomes obvious—not only in the architecture of the clocktower, but also in the two landward **Fortress Towers** erected by the Turks—whereas the **Citadel** and the **Sea Fortress** were built by the Venetians. The **Bastiana Restaurant** in Cavtat has a 'subsidiary' here operating under the same name. Three miles (5km) further south you will come upon the expansive spa and health resort of **Igalo**, with its hotels and sanatoriums for all types of ailments.

Kotor Bay reaches far into the mainland, and there is a ferry here which charges good money for the shortcut it offers. If you are travelling by car, however, you should reserve this option for the return journey. The longer route around the bay with the beautiful view of the two tiny islands and the steep mountain faces is well worth the effort. In **Risan** you can visit the remains of a Roman villa complete with third-century mosaics. This road then takes you by way of **Perast** to **Kotor**, the home of the oldest seamen's organisation. This brotherhood has proven itself in many a battle, even saving the Venetian fleet from a defeat in 1571 at the Battle of Lepanto. Since 1859 this seafaring 'gunclub' has been a strictly cultural organization. Every year, on the third of February, they celebrate the 'Festival of the Navy'.

Reaching high into the mountains, the **Town Walls** around the triangular heart of the Old Town present an impressive sight. Many precious pieces of architecture were severly damaged during an earthquake in 1979, but the **Tryphon Cathedral**, the **Church of Maria Collegiata** and **St Luke's Church** were all rebuilt with international help. The **Navigation Museum** of Montenegro located in the Baroque **Grgurin Palace** is worth seeing. The bay, which was considered virtually impregnable and was even barricaded with chains at its narrowest point, was used by many countries as a naval training centre. Both the Czar in St Petersburg and the Emperor in Vienna sent their cadets to Kotor.

From Kotor there is a road leading up to Lovćen, where a monumental **mausoleum** serves as the final resting place of the poet and prince bishop, Petar Petrović Njegoš II. The house where he

View of Kotor Bay

was born in **Njeguši** is a museum, but in order to get there, you must first get over the Trojica and Krstac Passes.

On the way to **Cetinje**—a city full of museums and memorials, but with few direction signs—you must overcome Bukovica Pass (elevation: 4,000ft/1,200m). The distance from Kotor to Cetinje is 28 miles (45km). The ascent to the Lovčen takes another half an hour by car, or taxi, and then there are still many, many stairs to be climbed, up through a broad tunnel. Once you have finally reached the top, however, the only thing missing is a pair of wings to make you feel like a bird soaring high in the sky. The clear view all the way to **Skutari Lake** and out over the rocky sea of high mountain peaks will take your breath away, as will the sight of the monumental sculpture of the poet in his mausoleum.

Arriving back down in the historic town of **Cetinje**, you should now be getting your bearings for **Budva**, 20 miles (32km) away. And, in case a high mountain tour does not appeal to you, or would foul up your schedule, then you can also reach Budva via the shorter route from Kotor. Then you need only follow the road signs when you get to **Trojica Pass**. **Budva**, too, was almost completely destroyed by the severe earthquake in 1979. The huge fort by the sea did the best job of withstanding the tremors. In the mean time, the town has been reconstructed according to old drawings and documents—during the process of which several interesting early historical finds were made.

A string of Montenegrine seaside resorts stretches all the way down to the Albanian frontier. Along this stretch of the Adriatic you will find **Ulcinj,** with its vast stretches of sandy beach, **Bar** and the crumbling pirate's hideout, **Stari Bar**, whose picturesque ruins are an attraction for photography buffs and romantic spirits alike. The one-time fishing village of **Sveti Stefan**, connected to the mainland only by a causeway, has been rebuilt as a luxury hotel, which prides itself in providing the international jet set with all the best things money can buy (Tel: 086-41333).

Nearby **Miločer**, steeped in tradition, is frequented by aristocrats, including the Serbian and Montenegrine royal families. Whether you are a monarchist or simply love bathing, Montenegro is definitely worth seeing. **Bar** is the terminus of the adventurous, modern train line connecting Belgrade with the Coast—and a journey through the Balkan ravines is certainly worth considering.

The excursions to Montenegro organised from Dubrovnik take at least one full day and only offer a fraction of what is described here. For information about tours, inquire at local travel agencies.

Tour 19

Ancient Epidaurum

By sea to Cavtat—once the ancient settlement of Epidauram.

After a stroll through the centre of Dubrovnik, why not treat yourself to a visit to the aquarium; or after an extensive tour of a museum, how about a relaxing boat outing? Down at the Old Harbour, forget about the throngs of swimmers crowding aboard the launches ready to take them to the sunning rocks on the Island of Lokrum. Instead, find a seat on one of the smaller boats heading along the Dubrovačka Zupa coastline to **Cavtat**.

The boats owners usually wait until their small barques have taken on enough passengers—some of them coming along only as far as Mlini, Srebreano or Plat, where they are spending their holidays. Hugging the shore, the leisurely trip past palaces and splendid hotels takes about an hour to reach its destination: the tiny harbour of Cavtat. The town, once the ancient settlement of Epidaurum, is said to have been the home of the first settlers of Dubrovnik. With its picturesque location between two coves, Cavtat has become a partly chic, partly family-orientated resort.

Cavtat

The main artery is a lively, park-style promenade with restaurants, cafés, boutiques and travel agencies, leading to the other shore at the opposite end. The landing stages there are where the Mediterranean cruise ships drop anchor.

In town, the former Residence of the municipal counts during the old Venetian days, the Baroque **Palace of the Captain**, is worth a visit. The building houses a rich library and an extensive collecion of old prints, as well as some interesting items of folklore. Other sights are the **Renaissance cloister** in the Franciscan monastery, the **Bogisic Museum**'s collection of paintings and, on the wooded hill rising out of the sea in front of the town, the **Mausoleum** of the ship-building Račić family, the work of sculptor Ivan Meštrovič dating back to 1920–2.

For dinner, I strongly recommend the **Bastiana Restaurant**—in fact, it would be a good idea to reserve a table as soon as you arrive (Tiha 9, Tel: 050-78312). The owner operates a fishing boat and serves the fresh catch in delightfully prepared dishes: try *scampi alla Buzara*. The wine menu includes the best the country has to offer, and you can catch the bus back to Dubrovnik at the stop by the bay—practically outside the restaurant door.

Dining Ex

Even along the Adriatic, food and drink hold body and soul together. Naturally, each region has its own special recipes. On the other hand, many of the names of so-called local specialities reveal their Italian origins.

Appetizers: *Pršut* comes from *prosciutto* and is a dried ham produced in excellent quality both in Istria and in the Dalmatian hinterland. *Pršut* is an essential ingredient of any Dalmatian hors d'oeuvres platter, as are the rich-yellow cheeses and olives. Pickled chillies and spiced *Kobasice*, salami-like sausages, are also often included. *Krvavice* are blood sausages made of innards and pig's heads—spiced according to the style of the region, but especially with garlic, thickened with cornmeal, boiled and then dried.

Soups and stews: Istrian *maneštra* is a light vegetable soup with ingredients which vary according to the season, flavoured with fat and herbs. *Jota* is a winter soup of beans, saurkraut and potatoes. *Lonac* means 'pot', and the contents depend on the time of year and geographic location. Usually it is a nourishing mixture of meat and vegetables. *Paštafažol* is the simplest stew along the coast; containing lima beans and thick noodles, it is eaten with bread.

Simple main dishes: *Peka* means that the 'pot' is placed over the pieces of meat and cut-up vegetables before they are placed in the hot coals of an open fire. *Janjetina pod pekom*, 'mutton under lid' is a very special treat. A lidded earthenware pot promises similar results but with more juice and vegetables. Depending on the particular dialect region, this variation of the chicken brick is called *'črijepna'* or *'šrepna'* and contains pheasant, turkey, any kind of wild fowl or rabbit. *Artičoke s bižima*

periences

i bobićem are artichoke hearts with broad beans, peas, young potatoes and all sorts of herbs. Add salt and oil to taste. *Blitva* is chard, cooked with plenty of garlic, an ideal side dish with fish and crayfish or with *Dalmatinska pržolica*. The latter is breaded beef, usually of good quality, on sauté onions—almost always a safe choice. Unfortunately, the chips (french fries) are often very greasy, literally floating in oil on your plate. *Blitvenat* is a baked casserole of chard and fresh cheese with raisins and dried figs. *Cicvara* is a bready side dish of wheat flour and cornmeal cooked with a little oil; many foods are also served with *pura,* thick, boiled corn semolina, or *polenta*, the lighter version.

Fish dishes: small dried anchovies in oil are a dainty delicacy together with wine or an appetizer. I also highly recommend a salad of marinated octopus: *salata od hobotnice,* also served using cuttlefish—but whether it be octopus, cuttlefish or squid, you will seldom go wrong ordering *mekušći na salatu*, shellfish prepared as a salad. *Buzara* is a sauce speciality, particularly used in the preparation of crayfish, prawns, lobster, and mussels. The standard in-

gredients are olive oil, bay leaves, white wine, onions, tomatoes, garlic, parsley and bread crumbs—everything else is derived from the cook's experience and is top secret. *Špageti na mornarskom* are noodles, prepared sailor-style with mussels and a fish broth. *Kamenice* are oysters—as are *oštrige*, by the way. *Dagnje* are mussels, as are *prstaci*, reddish-brown, date-shaped 'little fingers'. Unfortunately, breaded shellfish, grilled on a skewer, is not always available. You should try *Školke na štapiću*, if you happen to find it on the menu.

Fish from the grill, *na gradelama*, is done very tastily both along the coast and on the islands. Usually you can pick out the fresh fish yourself: brasse, perch, bass, mackerel and large sardines, as well as squid. Pike, codfish and 'devilheads' taste best *na lešo*, ie boiled or steamed.

Meat dishes: meat lovers can, of course, choose from the standard fare of *čebapčići* and *ražnići, pljeskavica* and pork shops. But as far as very typical dishes are concerned, I would like to recommend *pašticada*. It is beef from the leg, marinated and then spiked with cloves, fat and garlic—roasted on a bed of carrots, dried mushrooms and tomatoes. Other authentic specialities are: veal with sage, *govedina sa kaduljom;* or *sokoli*, pork neck which has been packed in salt for a week, pre-cooked in red wine and spiked with cloves, rubbed with cinnamon and pepper, then dried and finally served finely sliced with vegetables à la vinaigrette. And if risotto appeals to you, *crni rižot* is a black variation owing its name and appearance to the ink of the cuttlefish.

Pasta and desserts: noodles and dumplings are prepared in all kinds of ways. Doughnuts with raisins are usually served with powdered sugar. One popular dessert, *Rožata*, is a pudding made of milk and eggs covered with caramel sauce. Fruit, ice cream and many kinds of cake are listed on any menu.

Wines: I could go on forever about the wine. Each area here has good local table wines and quality wines with specified origins. Istria produces a good *Malvasier, Istarska Malvazija. Refošk* and *Merlot* are among the famous types. *Pinot, Teran* and *Kabernet,* likewise. Further south, the red types are better: *Plavac, Babić, Faroš, Dingač* and *Postup, Vranac* and *Blatina*. The white wines holding the top places on the wine list are: *Burgundac, Žlahtina, Malvazija* and *Grk, Maraština* and *Mostarska žilavka, Debit, Pošip* and *Vugava*.

There are a couple of terms to look for on the labels of the better sorts: *Cuveno vino* ('famous wine') and *Vrhunsko vino* ('premium wine'); these terms not only mean that the origin is certified, but also the particular wine is controlled and given a quality rating. *Kvalitetno vino s geografskim porijeklom* is the Croatian certification on quality wines with designated areas of cultivation and controlled quality; the Slovenian version reads: *Kakovostno vino z geografdkim poreklom. Stolno vino* is table wine, which is not to be scoffed at either. Many restaurants serve open wines, usually from the immediate vicinity. Generally, you will see the owner drinking these wines, as well, because the vineyard belongs to a relative or to a good friend whom he can trust.

Other drinks: as a starter, many people here like to drink a brandy, or *Lozovača*. Translated loosely, *Molim, jednu lozu*, means: "A grappa, please." To round off a meal you should have a small coffee, espresso or cappuccino.

Gemišt is half white wine and half mineral water, mixed. Red wine is also diluted upon request with tap water. Drunk with meals, this mixture, called *bevanda*, is quite popular even among the children. High-octane drinks are the fruit schnapps', *lozovaća* and *šljivovica*. The sweet, golden yellow *prošek* is a favourite dessert wine; amaretto, various bitters and brandies stand comparison with any of their kind; some even sport Italian-licensed names. *Travarica* is a speciality which is either industrially produced or else home made according to traditional methods. The process involves dousing aromatic and presumably medicinal herbs with spirits—*Rakija* is the word left over from the days of Turkish occupation. There are concoctions and household recipes for and against every ailment imaginable. *Travarica* is at its most attractive when the ingredients—herbs, twigs, leaves and berries—are left in the bottle.

Just one word of advice, though: try not to let the enjoyment get out of hand. Less is more. During the daytime, you might drink a glass of mineral water now and then, or order a fruit juice from the large variety available. That will keep you bright and lively for your social activities in the evening.

Calendar of Special Events

Yugoslavians also have their village festivities and fairs, special days dedicated to local saints and their altar paintings. To foreign guests the numerous concerts and folklore shows in the major cities along the coast may be the highlight of their holiday. In this section, I will briefly introduce a few of the many events and festivals—but beware of the fact that some of the large, internationally acclaimed festivals may be cancelled or crossed off the calendar of events permanently—due to a lack of funds.

The **Yugoslavian Feature Film Festival** is held at the end of June in the Arena in **Pula**. The **Yugoslavian Festival of the Child** in **Šibenik** brings

children and artists from all over the world together for two weeks at the end of July/beginning of August. New concepts must be found for both events—new financiers, as well.

The **Split Nights**—four very long Saturdays, cultural 'open nights' at the ends of June, July and August, respectively, as well as prior to 4 July, the Day of the Fighters—are so popular, that no one need fear for their future. Due to the tremendous rise in costs, however, the **Split Summer**, featuring concerts, opera performances and ballet at various spots around the Old Town, and the large **Pop Music Festival in Dubrovnik**, both from the beginning of July till the end of August, will most likely be subject to restrictions, as well, despite their large and faithful following.

Musical life in Dubrovnik is lively in the spring and autumn seasons as well; the **Musical Evenings of Osor** in July and August are special treats for visitors to the islands of Cres and Losinj.

The **Church Concerts** in **Sveti Donat** in Zadar attract connoisseurs of mediaeval music during the first two weeks in August and, in its Old Town of Varoš, **Zadar** witnesses one-day, massive **folklore festivals** in the middle of May, end of July and middle of September. The final weekend in May draws wedding couples from all over the world to **Plitvice** to get married in front of the large waterfall. And on the first Sunday in October, the large **Plitvice Marathon** is held.

In the towns at the foot of the Biokovo Mountains there are a few fixed dates with long traditions: there are **grill and folklore festivals** in **Baška Voda** on 1 May, on 27 July in **Tucepi**, on 10 September in **Podgora.** On 3 August there is a **pilgrimage** to the peak of the Sveti Jure at an elevation of 5,780ft (1,762m). On 8 August, **Makarska** celebrates its **Fishermen's**

Night with dancebands, folklore shows and a parade of decorated fishermen's boats.

Each 15 August, in Jelsa on **Hvar Island**, they commemorate the arrival of the Madonna Stomorena from Čitluk in the year 1539. If you are in Split, it is worth visiting the **Singers' Festival** in **Omiš** at the beginning of July, and the **mediaeval tournament**, the **Alka** of Sinj, on the first Sunday in August.

Each year, on 27 July, the **Moreška**, a mock fight over a noble lady, is danced on **Korčula Island**. On this same date, Kotor Bay is the scene of a **pilgrimage by ship**, the **Fašinada**. Shiploads of stones are dumped into the waters off the Church Island of the Madonna.

The above is by no means a complete list of all the celebrations and holidays—the political ones will probably disappear anyway or make way for other dates. Whatever town you are in, the locals will be glad to tell you what, when and where there is a celebration.

What to Know? Practical Information

TRAVEL ESSENTIALS

Entry

For a visit of up to 30 days only an identity card is required of citizens of most European countries.

Import Restrictions

As far as items for personal use are concerned, the import restrictions are applied quite generously—with only Yugoslavian citizens being checked more thoroughly. There are no restrictions on the import or export of currency.

Money Matters

In hotels and department stores you should have no problem paying either by Eurocheque, traveller's cheque or credit card—Visa and Eurocard being the most popular. And people everywhere are glad to change your money into 'dinars', the national currency. Officially there are restrictions on the amount of dinars you can import or export, but the guidelines are anything but up-to-date and realistic—in recent years the laws have been unable to keep up with inflation. In case you have already acquired a reasonable amount of 'spending money' either at home or on the way, no border officer is going to accuse you of violating exchange control regulations.

Electricity

Household electrical current is uniform throughout the country: 220 Volts AC at 50 hertz.

ABOUT THE COUNTRY

With its extreme contrasts, Yugoslavia is both bewildering and fascinating. Official texts dealing with the diversity of its population refer to "peoples and tribes". The largest group, the Serbians, make up about 41 percent of the total Yugoslavian population of 23 million people—followed by the Croatians with 23 percent, the Slovenes with 9 percent, the Moslems with 8 percent; the rest is made up by Macedonians, Albanians, Hungarians, Montenegrines, and numerous minorities such as Turks, Gypsies, Bulgarians and Italians.

The northern part of the coastal region is inhabited by Slovenes and Italians, the section between Istria and Kotor Bay by Croatians, whereas the southern area is populated by Montenegrines, whose history is closely linked to that of Serbia. Today, both its long state history and its dominant role in the Southern Slavic Union have put Serbia in a difficult position. On the one hand, the internal Slavic autonomies in Bojvodina to the north and in Kosovo to the south have practically been shelved; whereas, on the other, Serbia would like to establish the autonomy of its own large enclave within the Croatian Republic or—in the event of the transformation of the federation into a confederation—to have the respective border issue re-examined. Keeping these political vicissitudes in mind, let us turn to a more durable element: the landscape.

The **Dinaric Massif** stretches from **Istria** in the northwest to the **Albanian Alps** in the southeast. 188 miles (300 km) wide in its southern portion, this range covers just about half of Yugoslavia's total land area. Whereas the massif falls off rather gradually to the **Sava** and **Morava Rivers** in the interior, it presents an entirely different topography along the narrow **Adriatic Coastland**: the steep and partially precipitous mountain slopes of the **Velebit** (5,768ft/1,758m), the **Mosor**, the **Biokovo** and around **Kotor Bay**, all the way up to the **Durmitor** (8,275ft/2,522m) in the **heart of Montenegro** have a majestic beauty. Sometimes seeming even threateningly close, they

nonetheless provide a splendid backdrop for the pearls of the Adriatic: cities like Zadar, Šibenik, Trogir, Split, Dubrovnik and the islands offshore.

The huge longitudinal valleys and narrow basins running parallel to the Adriatic coastline are intersected by steep ravines: dramatic scenery which even fired the famous German adventure novelist Karl May's imagination, as well as attracting many a foreign film team. Up here in the **Uplands** mountain brooks sparkle, wild streams roar and huge lakes—many of them artificially dammed up and used to generate electricity—rest in their valleys. Quiet rivers teeming with fish wind their way down through green pastures before drying up in the **Karst.** Here and there the rivers are interrupted by waterfalls of a bizarre beauty—for example on the **Krka** and at the **Plitvice Lakes**.

The karst is a strange, impressive landscape. In the summer the whitish grey limestone is so dazzling it is painful, the air shimmers, the heat is hardly bearable. The meagre vegetation seems like a miracle, the sparse cultivated areas bearing corn, vines and vegetables are laid out in tiny plots of fertile red earth protected by stacked walls of stones. They are growing proof of the inhabitants' self-assertiveness. Drinking water is precious. Rain water immediately seeps away into the ground.

In the wintertime icy storms blow

in from the hinterland, racing across the karst with no forests to soften their impact—producing the feared *bora*. Its cold air masses stream down onto the coast land and the islands—sometimes causing severe damage, even sweeping cars off the coastal roads. A special warning to drivers pulling caravans: your light trailers could be blown away—literally sent flying off the road.

During the summer months the whole world is present along the Adriatic Coast from **Istria** to the Albanian border near **Lake Skutari**. Yugoslavia's most popular holiday destination is the highly varied coastal landscape and the offshore islands—the extensive middle section of which is **Dalmatia**. Although the summers on the coast are warm, the light sea breeze makes the heat more bearable and there is abundant water for swimming. Even the winters are quite mild, but usually unpleasantly damp. The Mediterranean vegetation consists of evergreen forests and, especially, of rampant brushwood or *macchia*. Beach pines, cypresses, stone oaks, plane trees and palms, olive groves and vineyards alternate in colourful variety. The trees are full of figs, almonds and carob, mulberries add colour to the pavement, while the nooks and crannies of the houses are verdant with greenery, with plants in jam buckets and flower pots.

Istria and Dalmatia still bear strong traces of the influence of Rome and Venice: cathedrals and town houses, fortress walls and palaces show evidence of this, as well as the language. Slovenian and, to an even greater degree, the coastal Croatian dialects have borrowed or preserved in modified form many terms from Italian. Even traditional music along the coast is living proof that a sea cannot separate people.

GETTING AROUND

Ferries/Shipping Lines

Ferries connect the adjacent coasts of the Adriatic. In addition to the busy marine traffic plying the waters between the mainland and the islands, you have the large shipping line ferries connecting Zadar with Trieste, Rimini and Ancona, Split with Venice and Pescara, Dubrovnik with Venice and Bari, and Bar, as well, with Bari in the south of Italy. Especially during the main season these ferries are a very popular means of transport. It is advisable to have a travel agent reserve both cabin and vehicle space well in advance of your travel date. The automobile clubs can provide information regarding prices and departure times.

Flying

During the summer there are numerous charter flights to airports on the coast and the interior. In addition to the state airline JAT, there is the Slovenian Adria Airways (formerly Inex-Adria), and the political turbulence could well bring about additional restructuring (the Croatians are considering starting up an airline of their own). Below you will find a list of all major airports offering international connections or domestic flights. For many travellers, Zagreb is a stopover or place to change planes, but the city also offers excellent bus connections and train services.

Zagreb:
Tel: 525511
JAT Zrinjevac 17
Tickets Tel: 436683

Ljubljana:
Tel: 25761
JAT Miklošičeva 34
Tickets Tel: 314340

Pula:
Tel: 24402
JAT Mate Balote 8
Tickets Tel: 23322

Rijeka:
Tel: 841133
JAT Putnička obala/Gat
Tickets Tel: 30207

Zadar:
Tel: 24444
JAT Natka Nodila 7
Tickets Tel: 436683

Split:
Tel: 551389
JAT Titova obala 8–10
Tickets Tel: 48070

Dubrovnik:
Tel: 23732
JAT Maršala Tita 7
Tickets Tel: 20055

Driving

Motorists vacationing in Yugoslavia generally cross the Alps, taking either the very steep Wurzen Pass to Podkoren or the slightly less steep Loibl Pass/Ljubelj. Drivers towing caravans or boat trailers should take the alternative via Graz and Spielfeld to Sentilj. Here traffic often backs up in the summer, but there are also several secret side routes and secondary border crossing-points—such as via Leibnitz, Ehrenhausen, Gamlitz and on narrow roads to the little-frequented crossing at Langegg to Jurski vrh. Do not forget to take a green insurance card for your vehicle, or you will have to take out third party insurance at the border.

Yugoslavia is still extending its network of **motorways**. The roadways are in good condition—however, a toll is charged. At present, motorists with foreign number plates pay twice as much as natives; the same regulation applies on the ferries to the islands.

The network of **filling stations** with unleaded petrol is satisfactory in the areas covered in this book. Purchasing petrol coupons at the border gives you a certain discount, but the authorities are contemplating the abolition of this measure.

Vehicle repair shops are occasionally prone to improvisation and there are also cut-throat breakdown services and run-down gyp-joints keen on making a profit out of someone else's unexpected misfortune. On the whole, though, my experiences have been positive—the unwritten obligation to help those in distress still means something in Yugoslavia.

Behind the wheel, however, the Yugoslavs are a reckless breed so that risky overtaking manoeuvres are quite the rule. The important thing is to remember to remain relaxed, keep a cool head and drive defensively. Or to paraphrase an Austrian traffic slogan: 'Avoid close calls—keep your distance.' If you are ever at a loss, call the **Automobile Club**. The emergency number of the AMSJ is the same throughout the country: **987**. 'Rent-a-car' is the established term for **car rentals**, Hertz being the number one agency.

Boat Charter

If you are interested in touring the coast in a large boat, I recommend you try any of the particularly well-equipped **ACY** yacht harbours. There is a central booking service for the ACY marinas and charter boats in Opatija (phone: 051-71206).

ACCOMMODATION

You will find lists of hotel addresses at the end of the respective tours of Pula, Tadar, Split and Dubrovnik.

For brochures on hotels and private lodgings including prices, please refer to any of the travel organisers' bureaux. There is a tremendous supply of hotel, boarding houses and private rooms, as well as apartments for rent. Any tourist office or agency branch will be glad to be of service and you cannot overlook the advertising and direction signs. You will even see 'Vacancy' signs posted outside tiny cottages along country roads. Admittedly, there is an element of adventure here, but I have rarely been disappointed by such wayside accommodation. I would not, however, recommend the crowded camping grounds along the Adriatic highway.

HEALTH & EMERGENCIES

The **hospitals** (*bolnica*) and out-patient clinics (*ambulanta*) provide good medical services—in fact, in the major centres there are even **tourist clinics** specialising in the quick treatment of minor ailments and accident injuries. You are advised to take along an **insurance certificate** from your own health insurance company or department of health—Yugoslavia has signed reciprocal health care arrangements with a large number of other countries. If you do not have health insurance or are not part of a medical plan, it is a good idea to take out appropriate

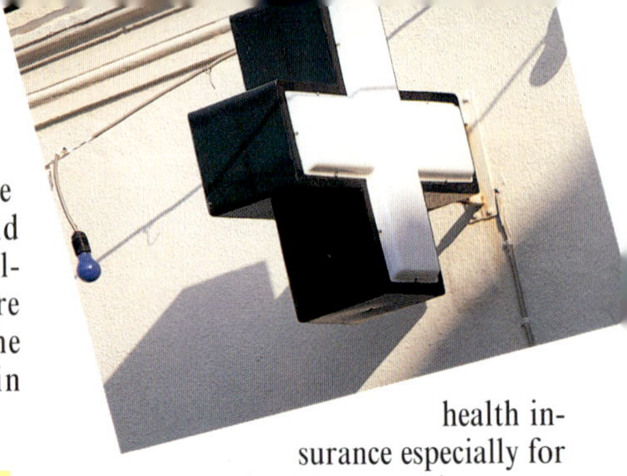

health insurance especially for your trip. Most vacationers are so healthy and cheerful that the importance of quick aid (*hitna pomoč*) never dawns on them—unless perhaps a sudden 'taa-too-taa-too' directs their attention to an emergency medical vehicle whizzing by. In the event of an unexpected attack of toothache or lost filling, you will need to ask for a dentist (or *zubar*, spoken with a very soft 's'!) and if you need aspirins or a sticking plaster, there is sure to be a chemist nearby (*lekarna* or *apoteka/apteka* or *lijekarna*).

SHOPPING

It is uncertain whether the large department store organisations and retail chains will survive the political-social changes, but the term *robna kuča* should help the usually friendly locals to put you on the right track—eg to the **Minčeta** or the **Srdj** at the Gruž Harbour in Dubrovnik, or to the monumental **Koteks** complex in Split, to the **Šibenka** in Šibenik or the **Dalma**, also in Split. You are best off letting a taxi take you there; they are not expensive and spare your nerves (providing you occasionally shut your eyes).

In addition to all sorts of souvenirs I would recommend the elegant **leather goods** and **handbags**, as well as the fashionable **clothing** on display in the many boutiques—very tastefully designed and often made by hand. **Records** and **tapes** of traditional and classical music are quite reasonably priced, whereas the products of the bands from the Yugoslavian rock and pop music scenes might have more oddity value. **Illustrated books** on the various cities and landscapes are weighty souvenirs and the accompanying texts are often poorly translated. This need not perturb you, however: you can quickly get an idea of their quality by skimming through a passage or two while you are in the shop. The work of **watchmakers** and **opticians**, **seamstresses**, **tailors** and **shoemakers** is usually in keeping with their traditional standards of good craftsmanship and a trip to the **hairdresser**—not necessarily the hotel hair stylist—is a way of getting not only careful hair (and moustache/beard) treatment but also of sampling local colour with the corresponding live soundtrack.

COMMUNICATIONS & MEDIA

Telephone

The call-boxes, which are also found mounted on the walls of buildings, require special **chips**, which you can purchase in any post office. They come in three different denominations: A, B and C. You wait in the box for a line, then dial the number and pay at the counter once you have completed your call. The reception of nearly every hotel provides the same service even to non-guests. You must be patient, however—the lines are so overloaded, particularly during the holiday season, that it may be midnight before you finally manage to get through to your family at home.

Tourist Information

If you intend to stay in a particular town for a longer period, it is worthwhile purchasing a small information pamphlet, a city guide or a detailed city map; up-to-date information, including the prices of hotel and private accommodation, is available at the travel agencies. They also offer calendars of events covering the dates of theatre and music festivals, art exhibitions, competitions and traditional celebrations, sporting events and conventions. And, of course, with the help of the hotel staff you should also be able to decipher enough of one of the very lively and varied daily newspapers to figure out who is putting on what when and where.

Press and Cinema

At a few of the news stands in the larger cities you will find a limited selection of foreign newspapers—especially from Germany, Austria and Italy, but also from further abroad. The kiosk racks are dominated by an array of tabloid newspapers and pulp magazines from the tourists' various home countries.

Movies are only shown in the original version with subtitles which, depending on the distributor, are either Serbo-Croatian or Croato-Serbian—ie, either more Serbian or more Croatian. Slovenian subtitles, found of course mainly in the north, are the exception.

Radio

Local and national radio stations not only provide the latest news in various languages, but also broadcast important traffic announcements and the current weather report.

Language

The language is the usual problem for most visitors, but the locals are so accustomed to dealing with foreigners that there is always bound to be somebody around to help out. Young people learn foreign languages in school, whereas the older inhabitants may have spent some time abroad—as foreign workers—and enjoy demonstrating what they learned in London, Manchester or Liverpool.

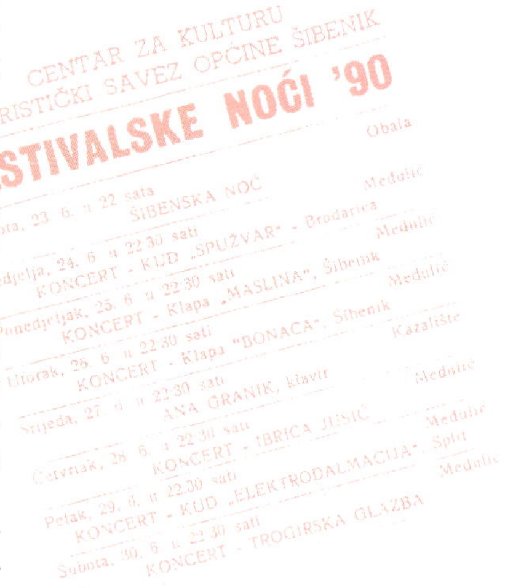

Index

K, L

M, N, O

P

Q. R

S

T, U, V

Art & Photo Credits

Photography **Oliver Lentz *and***
3 **Bill Wassman**
5, 96, 97B **Turistkomerc, Zagreb**

Cover Design **V. Barl**
Cartography **Berndtson & Berndtson**

NOTES

NOTES

Štanjel
Gorizia
SLOVENIJA
Reka
Ilirska Bistrica
Klana
Podhum
Rupa
Kraljevica
Crikvenica
Krivi Put
Gacka
ITALY
Vodice
Opatija
Rijeka
Omišalj
Senj
Krasno
Monfalcone
Trieste
Riječki Zaljev
KRK
Vrbnik
Jurjevo
1699
M. Rajinac
Malinska
Kras
Baska
PRVIC
JUGOSLAVIA
Krk
GRGUR
GOLI
Jablana
Koper
Gulf of Trieste
Porozina
Lopar
Rab
ISTRIEN
Raša
Merag
Kampor
Predošćica
Cres
RAB
Tovar
Pazin
Labin
CRES
Kvarneric
Buje
Višnjan
Vižinada
Savudrija
Umag
Barban
Zminj
Martinšćica
Koromačno
Novigrad
Osor
Poreč
Bale
Valle
Marčana
Zal. Raša
Kvarner
ZEČA
Unijski Kanal
Mali Lošinj
Rovinj
Barbariga
Pula
Medulin
UNIJE
Unije
LOŠINJ
Banjole
Susak
SUSAK
Vrata
Kvarnerićka
Adriatic

DINARA
Mostar
Peručko jezero
Buško jezero
Lištica
KOZJAK
Podosoje
Neretva
Buna
Aržano
Cetina
SVILAJA
Sinj
Imotski
Soviči
JUGOSLAV
IMOTSKO POLJE
Drniš
Čikola
Kljake
Lovreć
Ljubuški
Počitelj
Čaptina
Tasovčić
Zagvozd
Unešić
Kladnice
Klis
Sv. Jure
1762
Kozica
Vrgorac
Pisak
Metković
Omiš
Podgora
Makarska
Kaštel Stari
Kardeljevo
Split
Brački Kanal
Sumartin
Drvenik
Prapatnica
Sučuraj
Supetar
Trogir
Kruševo
Neretvanski Kanal
Trpanj
Hvarski Kanal
Bol
Županje Selo
ŠOLTA
BRAČ
Sv. Ilija
960
Maslinica
G. Selo
PELJEŠAC
Mljetski Ka
M. DRVENIK
V. DRVENIK
Lovište
Jelsa
Korčula
Govedjari
Polače
Mostir
HVAR
Korčulanski Kanal
Blato
KORČULA
Vela Luka
Viški Kanal
Lastovski Kanal
Lastovo
VIS
Vis
Uble
Komiža
LASTOVO
BIŠEVO

Jugoslavian Adriatic (North)

30km / 18.6 miles

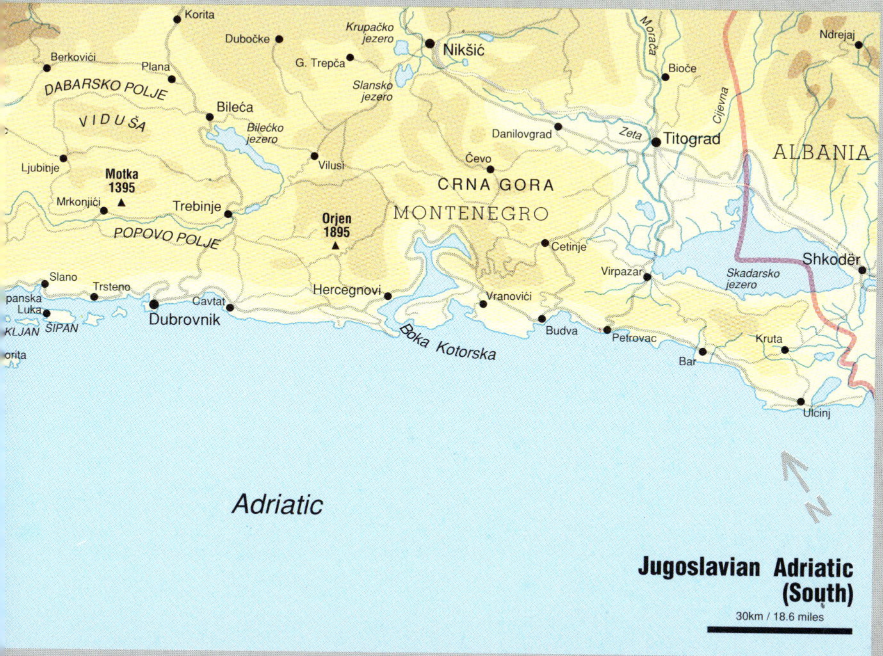

Jugoslavian Adriatic (South)

30km / 18.6 miles